CARTER G. WOODSON

IN

WASHINGTON, D.C.

The Father of Black History

PERO GAGLO DAGBOVIE, PHD

THE
History
PRESS

Published by The History Press
Charleston, SC 29403
www.historypress.net

Copyright © 2014 by Pero Gaglo Dagbovie
All rights reserved

First published 2014

ISBN 978-1-5402-1110-1

Library of Congress CIP data applied for.

In loving memory of my niece Melanie

She that dwelleth in the secret place of the most High shall abide under the shadow of the Almighty.
Psalms 91:1

One of the most inspiring and instructive stories in Black history is the story of how Carter G. Woodson, the Father of Black History, saved himself for the history he saved and transformed.

The skeletal facts of his personal struggle for light and of his rise from the coal mines of West Virginia to the summit of academic achievement are eloquent in and of themselves…

For in an extraordinary career spanning three crucial decades, the man and the history became one—so much so that it is impossible to deal with the history of Black people without touching, at some point, the personal history of Carter G. Woodson, who taught the teachers, transformed the vision of the masses and became, almost despite himself, an institution, a cause, and a month. One could go further and say that the systematic and scientific study of Black history began with Woodson, who almost single-handedly created the Association for the Study of Negro Life and History (now the Association for the Study of Afro-American Life and History) and the prestigious Journal of Negro History. *Not content with these achievements, he ventured into the field of mass education, creating annual Black history celebrations.*

What makes this so remarkable is that Woodson created these cultural monuments largely by his own efforts.
—Lerone Bennett Jr., 1999

CONTENTS

PREFACE

I wrote *Carter G. Woodson in Washington, D.C.: The Father of Black History* to serve as an accessible and brief book for all those interested in the life and contributions of Carter G. Woodson and the historical significance of the Carter G. Woodson Home, National Historic Site (NHS). This book should be especially useful to those who visit the Woodson Home and are further intrigued by its history and Woodson himself. From 1922 until 1950, Woodson's three-story Victorian-style row house in Washington, D.C.'s vibrant Shaw neighborhood, also called "Black Broadway," was the headquarters for the Association for the Study of Negro Life and History (ASNLH) and the Associated Publishers, Inc., as well as the epicenter of the early black history movement.

In a tribute to the man also known as the "Father of Black History," the Residence of the Phyllis Wheatley YWCA, 901 Rhode Island Avenue, Washington, D.C., declared: "We deeply appreciated having known Dr. Woodson, who was truly 'The House by the Side of the Road.'" These Washingtonians sampled from a famous 1899 poem by humanitarian, librarian and "common man" poet Sam Walter Foss to describe their humble friend who routinely ate dinner with them. The central character of Foss's poem happily lived "in a house by the side of the road," strove to help others and was, in essence, "a friend to man."

After earning a PhD in history from Harvard University in 1912 during an era of widespread Jim Crow segregation, Woodson played an unprecedented role in laying the foundations for the systematic study of African American history. An extraordinary organizer and motivator with a herculean work ethic (an eighteen-hour workday seemed routine for him), Woodson was a quintessential educational reformer and innovator who used history as an effective tool for generating wide-reaching social and cultural change. By the early 1920s, Woodson wholeheartedly devoted his life to maintaining the ASNLH, publishing scholarship on black American and Afro-diasporic history, training younger black scholars, popularizing black history and speaking out for blacks' civil rights. After he delivered the 1947 Founder's Day speech at Virginia Union University, Dean Gordon B. Hancock accurately dubbed Woodson "the high priest of Negro history."[1] The founder of Negro History Week (which developed into what we celebrate today as National African American History Month) in 1926, Woodson was, simply put, a black history institution builder.

Without reservations, I admit that I admire Woodson's accomplishments. At the same time, I acknowledge and recognize that above all else Woodson was a human being and a "complex, many-sided man." Described by a 1930 editorial in the *Afro-American* (Baltimore) as "the strange Harvard bachelor whose only true love has been his devotion to historical truth," Woodson himself acknowledged his peculiar personality. In the mid-1920s, he told one of his co-workers: "I suppose you have heard…that I am eccentric, that I do things in fits and starts."[2] Woodson was, indeed, no "ordinary" person. In the process of validating his people's past, he left his imprints deeply embedded within the walls of American culture. Historian Charles H. Wesley, the third African American to earn a PhD in history at Harvard University (in 1925), dramatically and effectually contextualized his elder's achievements in his 1951 essay "Carter G. Woodson—As a Scholar." Wesley observed:

We are almost too close in time to present an accurate view of Carter G. Woodson among scholars. The measure of the achievement of one whom we consider as a great scholar can be made with completeness not only by his work but also through the critical and creative achievements along similar lines of a subsequent generation of scholars. These scholars draw upon his discoveries and conclusions and build paths leading to truths. Smoller, the German historian, has stated that "History is in league with genius." In other words, as the nation and the people pass along the years, the individual and his work grow the greater. Then it becomes difficult to separate fact from fiction. The lives of the great men of American History have been of this pattern of developing halo and glory. Men and women who are often discounted or regarded as average persons develop with the passing years into those who are greater. Truly, in this respect, history is in league with genius.

This fundamental principle of our history makes itself manifest in the life and career of Carter G. Woodson. However, in his case we do not have to wait for the years to place him among the scholars, although we do not know how the future will rank all his historical writings. The discovery of new historical materials, the re-interpretations and the re-writing of history have led to re-appraisals of many a man's work. Nevertheless, we can now make our appraisal, with certainty, concerning Woodson. We do not have to ask for the fictionist, the poet and the builders of dreams to create his greatness. He has been a builder of his own monument.[3]

ACKNOWLEDGEMENTS

I am grateful to Robert T. Parker, the former site manager for the Mary McLeod Bethune Council House, NHS, and the Carter G. Woodson Home, NHS, for recruiting me to serve as the principal investigator for the historic resource study for the Woodson Home, NHS, from 2008 until 2010. The project was administrated and supported by the National Park Service, U.S. Department of the Interior and the Organization of American Historians. In 2010, I completed the historic resource study entitled *"Willing to Sacrifice": Carter G. Woodson (1875–1950), the Father of Black History, and the Carter G. Woodson Home, NHS.* According to the project's "Scope of Work," the objective of the study "is to synthesize cultural resource information from all cultural resource disciplines in a narrative designed to serve managers, planners, interpreters, cultural resource specialists, and the interested public as a reference for the history of the region and the resources within the park. The HRS supplies dates for resource management and interpretation, entailing both documentary research and field investigations to determine and describe the integrity, authenticity, associated values, and significance of resources." This book is a byproduct of the research that I conducted for this study.

Between January 2009 and July 2010, I received insightful feedback from National Park Service historians, the Association for the Study of African American Life and History's Carter G. Woodson Home Committee and a public historian employed by the Organization of American Historians. I thank Susan Ferentinos, Gary T. Scott, Elizabeth

Clark-Lewis, Bettye Gardner, June Patton, Sheila Flemming-Hunter, James Stewart, Daryl Scott, Sylvia Cyrus and V.P. Franklin for their support and feedback on drafts of the historic resource study that laid the foundations for *Carter G. Woodson in Washington, D.C.: The Father of Black History*. I also thank Banks Smither for his help and support as I prepared this book for publication.

A version of Chapter 2 previously appeared as "'Most Honorable Mention…Belongs to Washington, DC': The Carter G. Woodson Home and the Early Black History Movement in the Nation's Capital" in the *Journal of African American History*, volume 96, number 3 (Summer 2011): 295–34. I thank the editor and editorial board of the *Journal of African American History* for allowing me to reprint large portions of this article in this book.

"WILLING TO SACRIFICE"

*If a race has no history, it has no worth-while tradition, it becomes a
negligible factor in the thought of the world, and it stands in danger of being
exterminated...In such a millennium the achievements of the Negro properly
set forth will crown him as a factor in early human progress and a maker of
civilization...Let truth destroy the dividing prejudices of nationality and teach
universal love without distinction of race, merit or rank.*
—*Carter G. Woodson, 1926*

*Do not wait until the last moment to prepare for Negro History Week. The
time is nigh at hand. Secure the necessary literature at once and begin to plan
immediately to demonstrate to the community what you and your coworkers
have learned about the Negro during the year. For free literature write to C.G.
Woodson, 1538 Ninth St., N.W., Washington, D.C.*
—*Carter G. Woodson, 1940*

On March 23, 1945, Carter G. Woodson wrote to one of his
understudies and the driving force behind the early black history
movement in Missouri, Lorenzo Johnston Greene, praising him as being
"one of the few who appreciate the objectives" of the Association for the
Study of Negro Life and History (ASNLH) and who was "*willing to sacrifice*
something to attain these ends."[4] Embodying this "willing to sacrifice"
mantra, Woodson wholeheartedly dedicated his life to defining the scope
of the African American historical profession from the founding of the
ASNLH in 1915 until his sudden death in 1950. Woodson believed that

Most likely taken during the 1940s, this photograph suggests Woodson's confidence. *Courtesy of West Virginia State Archives.*

disseminating knowledge about black history was paramount to the black struggle for equality.

"Although he purportedly had several romantic and long-term relationships with women" and once "proposed marriage to a young lady" sometime between 1903 and 1907, Woodson remained a bachelor throughout his life.[5] "As a man with a cause, he was wedded only to his work and declared that no woman could stand his rigid regimen," Woodson biographer Sister Anthony Scally ascertained, "He lived in two rooms on the top floor of the Association's office on Ninth Street, where the basement was used as a warehouse for books. His dedication to the work of the Association absorbed him totally."[6] Remembering his mentor in the early 1970s, physical anthropologist and distinguished professor of anatomy at Howard University's College of Medicine W. Montague Cobb corroborated Scally's observations: "Dr. Woodson had no aversion to the ladies but he never married. He said he could not afford a wife. He even cautioned me against over-doing it in my earlier years, saying, 'You have a wife and children, Dr. Cobb, and you can't live like I live. I am a coal miner and I can take almost anything'…His bride was truly the Association and to her he left his worldly goods and his files."[7]

In a 1933 essay in the *Pittsburgh Courier*, "Carter G. Woodson Tells Reason Why He Never Married," Woodson explained his commitment to black history:

> *I have never married because, if I had done so, in my indigent circumstances my wife would not have a husband. When I began the work of the Association for the Study of Negro Life and History in 1915 I realized that I would have a hard struggle…I had to take the vow of poverty; and I did not proceed very far before I ran into so many unexpected difficulties that to continue the effort I had to take also the vow of celibacy…With the exception of twelve or fifteen dollars a week which I spend on myself and a smaller amount I give to a widowed sister, I turn back into the work all money which I can obtain…To be married under such circumstances would be out of the question, for I find that some of our modern women spend more than this amount in a moment for cigarettes and drinks.*[8]

No other individual has contributed as much as Woodson did to the development of African American history as an academic field of study, a conduit for American educational reform and a vehicle of black psychological and cultural liberation. The Woodson Home was designated a National Historic Landmark on May 11, 1976, and on December 19, 2003, Public Law 108-192 authorized the National Park System to acquire the building in order to incorporate it as a National Historic Site.

After decades of struggle to formally memorialize Woodson's contributions, on June 10, 2003, the Honorable Eleanor Holmes Norton, congresswoman from the District of Columbia, spoke passionately at the hearing before the U.S. Subcommittee on National Parks of the Committee on Energy and Natural Resources. She emphasized the profound significance of the Carter G. Woodson Home. In her "Prepared Statement," she proclaimed:

> *Mr. Chairman, I dare to say, there is not a Member of the House of Senate who does not commemorate in some way Black History Month annually in her state or his district. Yet, the home from which Dr. Woodson did his outstanding work here stands boarded up, as if to mock these celebrations. The Woodson home is a historic site because of the work that was done there and the influence of Dr. Woodson on American history and historiography and because his work helped bring changes in American attitudes concerning black people and ultimately changes in the legal status of African-Americans in our country...With the bill before you, an architectural landmark would be saved and preserved and the nation's pride and purpose in celebrating Black History Month would no longer be marred by neglect of the home of the founder of the commemoration and of the study of black history itself...Out of his Ninth Street home, Dr. Woodson trained researchers and staff and managed the organization's budget and fundraising efforts while at the same time pursuing his own extraordinary discoveries in African-American history. The three-story Victorian style house...served as the headquarters of ASNLH into the early 70's, well after Dr. Woodson's death in 1950. However, it has been unoccupied since the early 80's, and today, it stands boarded up and badly in need of renovation. The walls inside the house are crumbling, there is a termite infestation, water seeps through the roof during heavy rainstorms, and the house also constitutes a fire hazard jeopardizing adjacent buildings. This house is a priceless American treasure that must not be lost.*[9]

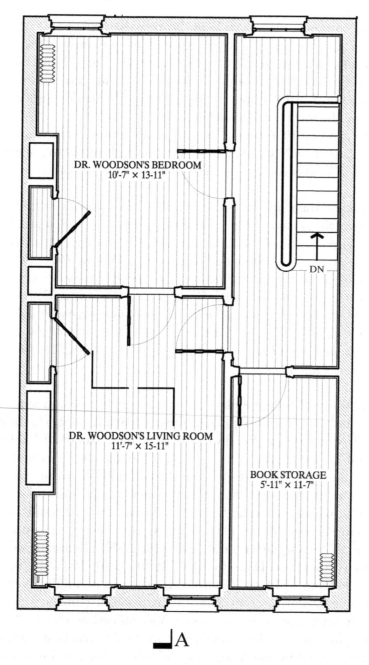

This floor plan for the third floor of the Woodson Home where Woodson lived was created by Robert R. Arzola based on the historic structure report by Beyer Blinder Belle, Architects and Planners. *Courtesy of the Library of Congress.*

Woodson's "office home," as Willie Leanna Miles dubbed the ASNLH's headquarters, was crucial to the success of the early black history movement that spanned from approximately 1915 until 1950. Woodson spent a great deal of time inside his 1538 Ninth Street, Northwest, residence between 1922 and the day of his death. He died peacefully in his bed on the third floor of his home.

In the January 1958 volume of the *Journal of Negro History*, under the heading "Historical News," Woodson's disciples challenged *Ebony* magazine's portrayal of Woodson's lifestyle. The *Journal* editorial staff wrote:

> Ebony Magazine *for February 1958 p. 27 contains the following regrettable sentence: "He had no home of his own, lived in rented lodgings as a boarder or ate out in restaurants." A sentence similar to this appeared in* Masses and Mainstream *for June, 1950. Both were flagrantly untrue and ridiculous! Dr. Woodson owned his home at 1538 Ninth Street, N.W., Washington, D.C., where he lived the last 30 years of his life and died. His meals were prepared to order at the Phyllis Wheatley Y.W.C.A. a half-block away! Moreover, he owned a 9-room home in Huntington, West Va., where his surviving relatives still live.*[10]

Woodson's office-home played a vital role in his mission to promote the scholarly study and popularization of black history. The building at 1538 Ninth Street, Northwest, housed the Associated Publishers, Inc. and served as the base of operations for the *Journal of Negro History*, the *Negro History Bulletin* and the ASNLH. Woodson wrote and dictated to his secretaries and stenographers numerous books, letters, memos, announcements and essays in the comfort of his office-home. Important figures of the early black history movement visited the association's headquarters, and during the ASNLH's annual meetings held in Washington, D.C., in 1917, 1919, 1920, 1925, 1929, 1933, 1937, 1942 and 1949, the "national office" was certainly a very busy place. The executive council of the association convened meetings there on more than a few occasions. The office-home at 1538 Ninth Street, Northwest, also functioned in other practical capacities. Books published by the Associated Publishers, Inc., and issues of the *Journal* and the *Bulletin* were stored in the basement and other spaces in the home along with other important documents. In his annual report for 1941, Woodson noted: "The Association...has on hand in its fireproof safe in the national office an additional 1,000 or more manuscripts which will be turned over to the Library of Congress as soon as they can be properly assorted. These manuscripts consist of valuable letters of the most noted Negroes of our time: Francis J. Grimké, Charles Young, Frederick Douglass, Booker T. Washington, and Richard Theodore Greerer."[11]

Equally important, the association's headquarters was in charge of overseeing association branches throughout the country and disseminating Negro History Week materials. Branches routinely corresponded with the "national office," and Woodson conceived of the branches as being "of service to the national office." Woodson received hundreds of letters at 1538 Ninth Street, Northwest, from schoolteachers, children and others interested in black history. Woodson routinely advertised the ASNLH's headquarters as being a clearinghouse of free information on black history and encouraged his readers to write to him. Under headings like "Negro History Week Literature Available Free of Charge" and "Negro History Week Literature Still Available," Woodson described 1538 Ninth Street, Northwest, as being a free reference bureau. For instance, in the *Negro History Bulletin* in February 1940, Woodson announced:

> *Some Negro History Week materials may still be obtained free of charge by writing Carter G. Woodson, 1538 Ninth Street, N.W., Washington, D.C. The demand has been so great that new supplies have been printed at the expense of the Association for the Study of Negro Life and History. This increasing demand is due to the fact that whites as well as Negroes are celebrating Negro History Week throughout the country.*[12]

Five years later, Woodson reiterated his offer, encouraging those interested in black history to take advantage of the resources housed at 1538 Ninth Street, Northwest. He wrote:

> *Literature for the celebration of Negro History Week, beginning February 10 and continuing through the 17th, will be available the first of December. Posters and information in other forms will be distributed free of charge. Send to the office of the Association for the Study of Negro Life and History your plans that you may have the fullest cooperation. The address is 1538 Ninth Street, N.W., Washington 1, D.C.*[13]

Woodson took great pride in noting that black history movements throughout the country were guided "under the stimulus and direction of the national office." Six months before he passed away, he highlighted the importance of the "national office" as an informational outreach center. "Research is the most important concern of the Association," Woodson wrote in his annual report of 1949, "When it is not working on any special project of its own it is, nevertheless, busy helping others thus engaged. Calls for such assistance from graduate students and their professors come daily to the national office."[14]

Quality scholarship has been published on Woodson. *Carter G. Woodson in Washington, D.C.: The Father of Black History* does not claim to be the authoritative study on Woodson. I did not write this book with an academic audience in mind. This book is intended to serve as a concise, straightforward introduction to Woodson's extraordinary accomplishments and vision of black history as well as the magnitude of the Carter G. Woodson Home, NHS. As such, it is largely free of academic jargon, theoretical formulations and historiographical debates.

Central to this study is (1) familiarizing readers with why Woodson has been called the "Father of Black History," (2) unraveling his "intricate" personality based largely on the recollections of those who knew him best, (3) highlighting the importance of Woodson's home as an early black history movement center, (4) discussing Woodson's relationship to the home, the Shaw neighborhood and the District of Columbia and (5) exploring how the usage of the Carter G. Woodson Home has evolved over time. In order to help reconstruct Woodson's persona, throughout this book I cite from Woodson's more obscure essays in black newspaper articles that previous scholars have not acknowledged.

Chapter 1 explores Woodson's life from his birth in New Canton, Virginia, on December 19, 1875, until his sudden death in his home on April 3, 1950. Chapter 2, the most extensive chapter, examines intriguing and previously under-acknowledged dimensions of Woodson's life and the ASNLH's activities in the nation's capital; the important role of the ASNLH's headquarters at 1538 Ninth Street, Northwest, Washington, D.C.; and the historical significance and evolution of the Carter G. Woodson Home, NHS. Chapter 3 showcases the various manners in which Woodson and the ASNLH popularized African American history. Chapter 4 features the recollections of Woodson's co-workers, employees, colleagues and disciples. Such reminiscences help us reconstruct Woodson's "intricate" personality. As one of his co-workers observed, "It is virtually impossible to evaluate a personality as intricate as that of Dr. Woodson," few "really knew him."[15] In the epilogue, I offer a personality trait analysis of Woodson that I hope is useful for those seeking to better understand his disposition. I also reflect on his legacy. This study includes a chronology; a list of the books written, edited and coauthored by Woodson; and a selected bibliography.

1

CARTER G. WOODSON, 1875-1950

Black History Institution Builder

In 1937, an editorial in the *Chicago Defender*, "The Personal History of a Historian: The Story of the Father of Race History Who Instructs a Class of Hundreds of Thousands of Students," pronounced:

> It is a feat for one who at 17 was just completing what is now regarded
> as an elementary education, to be acclaimed the greatest living authority
> on Race history at 62. Yet, that is the record of one of the greatest
> teachers of our time...Others, however—though perhaps not faced with
> the difficulties which confronted him—have done as much. But few there
> are living or dead who have contributed so much to the knowledge of the
> world as this great instructor...The man is Carter Godwin Woodson
> who was born of ex-slave parents...As he was one of the rather large
> family of nine children, his parents, who started life in poverty, could not
> provide him with ordinary comforts of life and could not regularly send
> him to the five months district school any longer than when he was old
> enough to work on the farm.[16]

In May 1920, Woodson wrote to Jesse E. Moorland:

> You should know enough about me to understand that I am the most
> independently hungry man in the United States. I once drove a garbage
> wagon in my home town, toiled for six years as a coal miner, often
> saw the day when my mother had her breakfast and did not know

Carter G. Woodson—Teacher, Historian, Publisher (1943) by artist Charles Henry Alston. This was part of a cartoon series promoting African Americans and "the War Effort." *Courtesy of the National Archives and Records Administration.*

where she would find her dinner. Many a time it was necessary for me to retire early on Saturday night that my mother might wash out the only clothing that I had that I might have something clean to wear the following day.[17]

A decade later, Woodson further explained how his humble beginnings impacted his drive. "A poor man can write a more beautiful poem than one who is surfeited. The man in the hovel composes a more charming song than the one in the palace." Woodson continued, "The painter in the ghetto gets an inspiration for a more striking painting than his landlord can appreciate. The ill fed sculptor live[s] more abundantly than the millionaire who purchases the expression of thought in marble and bronze."[18] When one considers Woodson's early years, his later accomplishments are nothing short of remarkable. He once told one of his understudies that he was "almost nineteen before he had learned the fundamentals of reading, writing, and arithmetic."[19]

About one century ago, Woodson began laying the foundations for the current advanced state of the study of African American history. He was the only individual of slave parentage to earn a PhD in history, and though W.E.B. Du Bois preceded him by close to two decades in earning a doctorate in history from Harvard University (in 1895), Woodson was the first professionally trained historian to devote his scholarly career to advancing black history as if he were involved in what he routinely called a "life-and-death struggle." He made great sacrifices for the cause of black history. As he testified to *Pittsburgh Courier* readers in 1933, he had to "take the vow of poverty" and made "every sacrifice to maintain the work of the Association for the Study of Negro Life and History."[20] During the peak of the Great Depression years, Woodson described his commitment to "the cause." In 1932, he noted:

> *I have never wanted wealth. I do not know what would become of me if I have to spend twenty-five thousand dollars a year on myself. I would rather have an allowance of twelve dollars and a half a week. The only need I have for money is to relieve the stress of others. It would take up too much of my valuable time to devise selfish schemes for throwing away a large fortune, and I would not have time to help humanity.[21]*

A year later, Woodson added:

> *In the sphere in which we are working there is no possibility for adequate compensation. The Association for the Study of Negro Life and History cannot pay men according to what they are worth. We have never had a staff of six or seven employees receiving four and five thousand dollars each annually.*
>
> *In the work of the Association an employee is supposed to catch the spirit of the organization and give his time and labor for a mere pittance. At present I am paying an employee on my staff twice as much as I receive because he has more dependents than I have; and, although he*

has been offered elsewhere more than he received from the Association, he remains with us.

Several persons have said to me that you are doing your work at too great a sacrifice, for the public should do more to support it...Yet I do not think that any of our workers feel that they should be praised for what they have done. These sacrifices have been willingly made. These workers who make such sacrifices for the good of others are doing what all Negroes in the service of their people must learn to do if the race is to be extricated from its present predicament.[22]

In 1930, one of Woodson's disciples was amazed with Woodson's commitment to his cause. "His [Woodson's] capacity for work is certainly outstanding. Eighteen hours a day seems to be routine for him," Lorenzo J. Greene noted in his diary, "He does everything from writing books, editing the *Journal*, wrapping books, mailing letters and parcels. Nor is he above acting as a janitor and sometimes his own cook. Truly a remarkable man."[23] Two decades later, Harlem Renaissance poet-activist extraordinaire Langston Hughes echoed Greene's observations. Hughes recalled:

In the mid-1920's when I worked for Dr. Woodson, he set an example in industry and stick-to-it-tiveness for his entire staff since he himself worked very hard. He did everything from editing The Journal of Negro History *to banking the furnace, writing books to wrapping books. One never got the idea that the boss would ask you to do anything that he would not do himself. His own working day extended from early morning to late at night. Those working with him seldom wished to keep the same pace. But he always saw that we had enough to do ahead to keep our own working hours entirely occupied.*

One time Dr. Woodson went away on a trip which those of us in his office thought would take about a week. Instead, he came back on the third day and found us all in the shipping room playing cards. Nobody got fired. Instead he requested our presence in his study where he gave us a long and very serious talk on our responsibilities to our work, to history, and to the Negro race. And he predicted that neither we nor the race would get ahead playing cards during working hours.

My job was to open the office in the mornings, keep it clean, wrap and mail books, assist in answering the mail, read proofs, bank the furnace at night when Dr. Woodson was away, and do anything else

This photo of Langston Hughes was taken by Gordon Parks in 1943. Hughes worked for Woodson briefly in the 1920s. *Courtesy of the Library of Congress.*

that came to hand which the secretaries could not do…It may be said truly of Dr. Woodson that never did anyone with so little bring self-respect to so many.[24]

Many who knew Woodson reiterated Greene's and Hughes's sentiments. From the late summer of 1922 until the day of his death, Woodson worked out of his office-home at 1538 Ninth Street, Northwest, in Washington, D.C. One of Woodson's close co-workers "never knew Woodson to miss a day from the office because of illness."[25] Woodson's unrelenting work ethic took its toll on his physical well-being and may have even contributed to his sudden death. In response to rumors that his health was failing in 1926, Woodson announced to readers of several leading African American newspapers that he was healthy. "A physician did tell me sometime ago that if I did not go more slowly I would kill myself soon," he acknowledged. But Woodson dispelled the hearsay: "I am working myself to death for the Negro, but my health is generally good."[26]

Woodson's life was similar to the lives of many famous African Americans that overcame seemingly insurmountable odds and obstacles to achieve monumental feats. Though born during the era of Reconstruction, his early years were similar to those of one of his ideological mentors, Booker T. Washington, who rose "up from slavery."

The circumstances of Woodson's early years and upbringing clearly influenced the course of his life after he earned his PhD from Harvard University in 1912. In 1985, librarian Sister Anthony Scally commented: "Anyone writing about Carter G. Woodson discovers how difficult it is to find accurate materials." This Woodson biographer added, "Most of the accounts of Dr. Woodson contain errors of fact, not yet of great importance, indeed, in assessing the undoubted value of his work, but annoying and puzzling to the researcher."[27] In reconstructing the important dates, events and experiences in Woodson's life, I have found that there is a range of interpretations. Scally and historians Jacqueline Goggin and Patricia Romero, among others, have offered more than a few different specific dates for certain events in Woodson's life.

Part of the problem facing Woodson's biographers is that he never wrote an autobiography. Though he did once say that he would someday "write a short autobiography," he only authored two significant autobiographical essays.[28] In a 1932 essay printed in the *New York Age* and the *Chicago Defender* ("And the Negro Loses His Soul") and a 1944 article in the *Negro History Bulletin* ("My Recollections of Veterans of the Civil War"), Woodson provided some important details of his early life experiences.

Woodson was born in New Canton, Virginia, in Buckington County on December 19, 1875. His parents, James Henry and Anne Eliza (Riddle), were former slaves and shared with him firsthand recollections of life during slavery. His father told him how he had physically overpowered his master to take his freedom. He instilled within his son a sense of nonconformity. Woodson's father was hired out by his owner and created a life within the restrictive institution of slavery, learning how to fish and make furniture. During the Civil War, he worked as a contraband behind Union lines. Later in his life, Woodson commented that his father's stories

Anne Eliza Riddle Woodson, mother of Carter G. Woodson. *Courtesy of West Virginia State Archives.*

sparked his later interest in documenting the memories of ex-slaves. As a professional historian, Woodson stressed the importance of documenting and recording the personal life histories of everyday people. He often instructed black youth during Negro History Week to interview their

Woodson's sister Bessie Yancey Johnson Woodson. *Courtesy of West Virginia State Archives.*

elders and document the histories of their families and communities. Woodson came from a large family, nine children in total, including his two siblings who died from a whooping-cough epidemic. Woodson's literate mother and his father raised their children to value education, a firm moral code and upright living.

In 1932, in the *Chicago Defender* and the *New York Age*, Woodson recounted the notions of self-sufficiency, dignity and elementary black nationalism that he learned from his father. Woodson recalled:

> *From my father…I learned better…He had been a field slave and could neither read nor write, but he proved to be the greatest factor in my education…This former slave, an illiterate man, taught me that you do not have to wait until you die to think of losing your soul. He insisted that when you learn to accept insult, to compromise on principle, to mislead your people, you have lost your soul…He taught his children to be polite to everybody but to insist always on recognition as human beings; and, if necessary, fight to the limit for it. Do not do for the traducer of the race anything he will do for you. Do not curry his horse, and grin at him for a favor. Do not brush his hat with one hand while holding the other for a tip. Do not clean his spittoons for the pittance which he offers. Do not serve in his kitchen for the refuse from his table. Do not shine his shoes to get the wornout ones for yourself…He often said to me, "I had to do these things when I was a slave. If I continue to do them, I am not a free man. If you do these things you cannot look the oppressor in the eye and say, 'Sir, I am your equal.' Neither he nor you will believe it"…In spite of this poverty, however, my father believed that such a life was more honorable than to serve some one as a menial. While his children were under his vine and fig tree, then, he never hired one to anybody; he never permitted one to wear anyone's cast-off clothing; and he never permitted one to go to any man's back door.[29]*

A year before Woodson's birth, his parents purchased a home and farm in New Canton, Virginia. As a child, Woodson grew up on his father's farm. Like many black youths coming of age during the immediate post-Reconstruction period, or "the Nadir," he attended a rural school for only about four months out of the year. "When he learned to read, his father required him to read to him every day from whatever discarded newspaper they could salvage. It was stale news, but a small window on a wider world."[30] His family worked hard in order to make ends meet.

Woodson labored on the family farm until he was about fifteen. He grew up very poor, as he recounted in 1932:

> *Often I remember that I had only one garment and had to go to bed early on Saturday night that my mother might wash this and iron it over night. In this way only I would have something clean to wear to Sunday school. Often during the winter and early in spring we did not have sufficient food, and we would leave the table hungry to go to the woods and pluck the persimmons which the birds had pierced with their beaks and left on the trees. Sometimes in the fields we had to eat the sour grass that grew early in spring out of the providence of God.*[31]

In the early 1890s, he hired himself out as a farm and manual laborer, and he drove a garbage truck in Buckingham County, Virginia. In 1892, Woodson moved to Fayette County, West Virginia, to work in the coal mines. This was certainly hard and dangerous work. A piece of slate once fell on him, causing an injury to his head. Woodson's years toiling in the coal mines left a deep impression on him. Willie Leanna Miles remembered that when she worked in the ASNLH office during the 1940s, Woodson ritualistically told visitors about his experiences in the coal mines. "I am a coal miner and I can take almost anything," Woodson often reminded his co-workers. Even with a PhD from Harvard University, Woodson held on to his working-class, coal miner identity. He took great pride in his poor, working-class background. This perhaps helps explain his drive to make the work of the ASNLH relevant to the lives of everyday black people. In a sense, he knew from firsthand experiences what the masses of black people were going through. In the early 1940s, Woodson argued that blacks would advance in America only with the leadership of "the laboring classes" since they were "not obligated to the oppressors of their people" as were their spokesmen or "hand-picked agents."[32]

Looking back on his life in his late sixties, Woodson also described his early years as being very significant to his intellectual development. While working in the coal mines, he met a black Civil War veteran named Oliver Jones. "He was well educated," Woodson recalled, "but could neither read nor write." Jones allowed many of the coal miners to use his home as an informal school. Being the sole literate worker of the group, Woodson read newspapers to his co-workers as he had done and would later continue to do for his father. Jones also had a valuable library of

African American miner picking coal out of the narrow seam (5.5 feet), Brown Mine in Brown, West Virginia. 1908. Photography by Lewis Wickes Hine. *Courtesy of the Library of Congress.*

books containing classic works by pioneering self-trained black historians like George Washington Williams, J.T. Wilson and W.J. Simmons. In his autobiographical essay "My Recollections of Veterans of the Civil War," Woodson credited Jones with igniting his interest in historical research. "I learned so much because of the more extensive reading required by him than I probably would have undertaken for my own benefit," Woodson recounted. "My interest in penetrating the past of my people was deepened and intensified." He added: "In this circle the history of the race was discussed frequently, and my intent in penetrating the past of my people was deepened and intensified."

Before becoming a professionally trained historian, Woodson's views of black history were influenced by those self-trained black scholars active during the last several decades of the nineteenth century like William Wells Brown, Joseph T. Wilson and especially George Washington Williams (1849–1891). In a 1945 article, "Negro Historians of Our Times,"

George Washington Williams (1849–1891), dubbed the "first" African American historian by John Hope Franklin, is most famous for his *History of the Negro Race in America from 1619 to 1880* published in 1882. *Courtesy of Wikimedia Commons.*

Opposite, top: Students at Berea College in Berea, Kentucky, circa 1899. *Courtesy of the Library of Congress.*

Opposite, bottom: "Filipino children outside a native school house, Philippine Islands" (1906). *Courtesy of the Library of Congress.*

Woodson praised Williams. "Williams' *History of the Negro Race* has not yet been superseded by a better work, and *History of Negro Troops in the War of the Rebellion* far surpasses any other work on this subject," he surmised.[33]

At the age of twenty in 1895, Woodson returned to Huntington, West Virginia, to live with his parents and attended Frederick Douglass High School, for which he would later serve as principal in the early 1900s. From 1895 until 1897, he attended Frederick Douglass High School. In the fall of 1897, he ventured to the abolitionist-founded Berea College in Kentucky. He eventually received a baccalaureate degree from Berea on June 3, 1903. For financial reasons, he left Berea after about a year, and from 1898 until 1900, he worked as a teacher for a school in Winona, West Virginia, where he educated the children of black miners.

In 1922, Woodson remarked that black West Virginians became excited in education during his teaching days in Winona and that "often Negro children in groups of only four or five were thus trained in the backward districts, where they received sufficient inspiration to come to larger schools for more systematic training."[34] Woodson was one of those teachers who helped inspire this thirst for learning. From 1900 until 1903, he returned to his high school alma mater, Frederick Douglass High School, teaching history and serving as the principal. Woodson was in his mid- to late twenties and already the principal of a high school. Woodson also remained close to his parents during these years.

After receiving a bachelor's degree in literature from Berea in the summer of 1903, from mid-December 1903 until early February 1907, Woodson traveled abroad. For roughly five years under the auspices of the U.S. War Department, he went to the Philippines "to train the Filipinos to govern themselves," teaching English, health and agricultural classes. With an impressive salary of one hundred dollars per month, he first arrived in Manila in late December 1903. He was first assigned to work in a country town in Nueva Ecija Province "among simple people tilling the soil and growing crops." In June, he was reassigned to another province, Pangasinan, where he trained Filipino teachers. He enjoyed this work very much and remained there until he resigned due to sickness early in 1907.[35]

Woodson wrote about his experiences in the Philippines in *The Mis-Education of the Negro* (1933). He believed that the most effective way to educate the Filipinos was based on their own history and culture. He went to the Philippines not as a typical missionary, but as a culturally sensitive reformer. While there, Woodson also mastered French and Spanish, skill sets on which he would later draw when reading, collecting and reviewing European scholarship on Africa. After leaving the Philippines in early 1907, Woodson briefly traveled around the world to Africa, Asia and Europe, spending roughly half of a year in Europe. He briefly attended the Sorbonne in Paris, France. There he studied European history, which most likely helped widen his scope of knowledge preparing him for his studies at the University of Chicago and Harvard University and, later, for the writing of many book reviews in the *Journal of Negro History* dealing with European subject matter.

After returning from Europe, Woodson enrolled in the University of Chicago, and a year later, he received a master's degree in history, romance languages and literature in the late summer of 1908. His MA thesis, "The German Policy of France in the War of Austrian Secession," was far removed from the African American experience. Woodson then enrolled in Harvard University as a doctoral student, and he briefly lived in a graduate dormitory. In 1909, he left Cambridge and settled down in the Washington, D.C. area in order to teach, first at Armstrong Manual Training School. He then taught French, Spanish, English and history at the prestigious M Street High School. Woodson conducted research, completed his comprehensive examinations and wrote his dissertation while working as a teacher full time. Professors in Harvard's history department did not share Woodson's interest in black history.

Woodson took classes from Edward Channing. Albert Bushnell Hart, W.E.B. Du Bois' former advisor, served as his advisor. Woodson completed his course work in less than two years and submitted the first draft of his dissertation in the spring of 1910. His dissertation committee, consisting of Hart, Channing and Charles Haskins, offered many suggestions for revision. By January 1911, he had finished the revised draft. After finally passing his American history comprehensive examination in April 1912, Woodson completed his PhD dissertation, entitled "The Disruption of Virginia." His study was worthy of publication, but he did not receive the necessary support to do so.

Woodson did not talk extensively about his experiences at the University of Chicago or Harvard. He did not seem to enjoy residing in "the North." Like Booker T. Washington, on several occasions he portrayed northern cities as conduits for immoral behavior. In a 1932 essay in the *Pittsburgh Courier*, he recalled: "In the dormitory in which I lived in a northern university the students had a 'beer night' twice a week, and there was a national prostitute on the stage who boasted that she had spent nights in every men's dormitory on that campus."[36]

In 1912, Woodson became the second African American to earn a PhD in history in the United States, following in the footsteps of W.E.B. Du Bois, who had earned his PhD from Harvard seventeen years earlier. Though both encountered racism at Harvard, their experiences were different, as were their views of black history. While Du Bois excelled at Harvard, Woodson struggled. They produced different genres of black historical scholarship. Du Bois was especially critical of Woodson's approach to history. While he dubbed Woodson's *The Education of the Negro Prior to 1861* "the most significant book concerning the Negro race" published in 1915, Du Bois was outspoken in his critique of Woodson's *The History of the Negro Church* (1922). "Mr. Woodson is a monographist of the strict Harvard dry as dust school" who "has collected and carefully catalogued and pigeonholed an enormous number of facts concerning American history," Du Bois wrote in the *Freeman* in 1922.[37] Certainly impacted by their divergent experiences with the Phelps-Stokes *Encyclopedia Africana* project, Du Bois wrote a mean-spirited obituary for the "Father of Negro History" in *Masses and Mainstream.*

Scholars have offered a range of explanations as to what sparked Woodson's decision to devote his life to the study of black history. Woodson's experiences at Harvard appear to have been pivotal. It was there, Woodson told one of his protégés, where he received, "in a negative way, the inspiration for his life's work." While attending one of the classes of longtime Harvard professor and renowned American historian Edward Channing, "he listened in amazement at the eminent Professor who told the class that the Negro had no history." Woodson told Lorenzo J. Greene that he challenged Channing and retorted that "no people lacked a history." According to Greene's account, Channing then told Woodson to prove him wrong. Woodson then "accepted the challenge" and "resolved to ascertain whether he or Channing was correct."[38]

The mid- to late 1910s were vital years in Woodson's career as a historian. At the age of forty, in the spring of 1915, Woodson published his first monograph, *The Education of the Negro Prior to 1861*, a densely footnoted monograph that he had worked on during and following his doctoral studies. According to historian Earl E. Thorpe, *The Education of the Negro Prior to 1861* was one of Woodson's "most scholarly [works] from the standpoint of documentation and general objectivity." Woodson analyzed the educational opportunities for African Americans in the antebellum

This is a photograph of W.E.B. Du Bois as he appeared in 1919. *Courtesy of the Library of Congress.*

era in two major periods: the introduction of slavery to 1835 and 1836 through about 1861. For Woodson, the history of African Americans and education during the antebellum era was largely a story of the "reactionary" tendencies of whites to blacks' struggles for education. Woodson's first book was reviewed positively in more than a dozen journals.

In the same year that his first major publication appeared, Woodson began institutionalizing the study of black history. On September 9, 1915, Woodson co-founded the Association for the Study of Negro Life and History (ASNLH) in Chicago with George Cleveland Hall, James E. Stamps and Alexander L. Jackson. At the first biennial meeting of the ASNLH, the executive council amended and ratified the association's constitution. The purpose of the organization was clearly spelled out: "Its object shall be the collection of sociological and historical documents and the promotion of studies bearing on the Negro."[39] The executive council was in charge of approving people to become members of the association. The annual membership fee was initially one dollar, and a life membership was initially thirty dollars. By the early 1920s, active members paid three dollars a year, and life members paid fifty dollars. By 1926, a life membership was seventy-five dollars. The officers of the ASNLH were similar to those of other such organizations and included a president, a secretary-treasurer, a director of research, an editor and an executive committee.

Ten years after founding the association, Woodson reiterated the purpose of the organization: "It proclaimed as its purpose the collection of sociological and historical data on the Negro, the study of peoples of African blood, the publishing of books in this field, and the promotion of harmony between the races by acquainting the one with the other."[40] Two decades after founding the association, Woodson defined the organization as a group of intellectual policemen:

> *The Association for the study of the Negro is standing like the watchman on the wall, ever mindful of what calamities we have suffered from misinterpretation in the past and looking out with a scrutinizing eye for every thing indicative of a similar attack. The staff, then, must be so enlarged and made so efficient as to furnish on short notice a scientific appraisal of any work on the Negro in America or abroad. A special service in this field is now being rendered by the quarterly publication of such bibliographical survey in the* Journal of Negro History, *and this will be extended to cover scientific productions in other areas.*[41]

During Woodson's lifetime, the association had five presidents: G.C. Hall, Robert E. Park, John R. Hawkins, John Hope and Mary McLeod Bethune. From 1915 until 1950, Woodson was director of research and editor and was involved in all the important decision-making processes of the association. Throughout the 1920s, 1930s and 1940s, Woodson referred to the association as a "scientific" (i.e., rigorously academic in nature) organization that sought to unite "the efforts of both a learned society and a bureau of research," employing "investigators to explore fields of Negro history hitherto neglected or unknown." Woodson welcomed lay historians, ministers, secondary and elementary schoolteachers, businessmen and the African American community as a whole into the ASNLH. The association developed close ties with black communities. During Woodson's lifetime, the association meetings were regularly held in black churches, community centers, colleges and universities and high school auditoriums throughout the country.

Though actively supported by various white philanthropists from the 1920s through the early 1930s, Woodson regularly sought the support of the black masses, especially after he formally severed ties from white philanthropists in 1933. Woodson directly told *Journal of Negro History* readers and subscribers how they could help the early black history movement. The following statement routinely appeared in the front matter of the January volumes of the journal beginning in 1918:

> *Five Ways to Help This Cause:*
> *Subscribe to the* JOURNAL
> *Become a member of the Association*
> *Contribute to our Research Fund*
> *Collect and send us the historical materials bearing on Negroes of your community*
> *Urge every Negro to write us all he knows about his family history*

Woodson also called on the black community to help fund the association in more direct manners. He outlined how the association's work could be more effective if the black community collectively contributed to its financial stability. In the following plea from 1932, Woodson candidly informed journal readers why the association needed substantial financial resources in order to fulfill its mission:

> *$30,000 NEEDED*
> *Help us raise annually the sum of $30,000 to finance the work of collecting and publishing the materials bearing on Negro life and history. Our efforts have hitherto been restricted to what we have been able to induce interested individuals to undertake in their respective localities.*

Moving at this slow rate and in such an unsystematic way, the work will proceed so slowly that many valuable documents and the testimonies of slaves and masters will be lost to the world and the story of the Negro will perish with him.

To raise this fund we are appealing to all persons professing an interest in the propagation of the truth. We need
4 persons to contribute annually $1,000 each
8 persons to contribute annually 500 each
16 persons to contribute annually 250 each
20 persons to contribute annually 100 each
40 persons to contribute annually 50 each
80 persons to contribute annually 25 each
200 persons to contribute annually 10 each[42]

In 1916, Woodson singlehandedly launched the first issue of the *Journal of Negro History*, the first major historical journal of the black American experience. The journal addressed a wide range of issues pertaining to Afro-diasporic histories, especially dealing with African American history. By 1919, the journal reached 4,000 people. In 1919, Woodson maintained that there were 1,648 subscribers, that six hundred copies were sold at newsstands and that five hundred bound copies, including all four volumes in a single volume, were sold. As tributes reprinted in the *Journal of Negro History* in 1966 under the heading "Fiftieth Anniversary of the *Journal of Negro History*" revealed, Woodson's scholarly journal was praised by a diverse group of scholars, black and white.

In 1918, Woodson became the principal of Armstrong Manual Training School in Washington, D.C., where he advocated vocational and classical education. While serving as principal at Armstrong Manual Training High School, Woodson published his second major monograph, *A Century of Negro Migration* (1918). A year later, he employed J.E. Ormes, formerly in the business department of Wilberforce University, as a field agent to increase membership of the association, appoint agents to sell books and subscriptions to the journal and organize black history clubs. In the early years, Woodson called on any interested individuals to join his cause. In 1919, Woodson announced that "any five persons desiring to prosecute studies" in black history could organize a club. Each club was required to pay the association two dollars, which entitled the club to a year's subscription to the journal and access to Woodson, by mail, for advice and the necessary instruction. He often sent clubs bibliographies and outlines for study. Woodson mandated that the clubs elect a president, a secretary, a treasurer and an instructor, the group's "most intelligent and the best informed member."[43]

In 1919, Woodson completed his important monograph *The Negro in Our History*. "While it is adapted for use in the senior high school and freshman college classes," Woodson noted, "it will serve as a guide for persons prosecuting the study more seriously." Woodson planned to send field agents to "Negro schools of secondary and college grade" in order to arouse interest in this first major textbook in African American history. However, because of what Woodson called a "printer's strike," *The Negro in Our History* was not published until 1922.[44] The foundations for Woodson's devotion to the black history movement were laid during the Progressive era. By the early 1920s, Woodson had fully dedicated himself to the ASNLH and the promotion of African American history.

While being active in the early black history movement, Woodson was also active as a history teacher. Like Booker T. Washington did at Tuskegee Institute, Woodson also inaugurated an adult education program at Armstrong Manual Training School. From 1919 until 1920, he served as the dean of Howard University's School of Liberal Arts, introducing and teaching black history there at both undergraduate and graduate levels. Like Charles Hamilton Houston, who added innovations to the Law School at Howard, Woodson established graduate training in history there. He was known among students for his seriousness and high expectations. Arnett Lindsay, Woodson's first successful graduate student at Howard, recalled how rigorous the training was that he received under Woodson's guidance.

Woodson did not see eye to eye with the white dominated administration and left Howard after one year of work. Many of his indictments of black colleges in *The Mis-Education of the Negro* (1933) originated from his experiences at Howard. Woodson was outspoken in his criticism of Howard's President J. Stanley Durkee. In 1925, he refused to participate in a program at Douglass High School in Baltimore, Maryland, because Durkee was also scheduled to speak. "I would not disgrace myself by appearing on the same platform with any man who has insulted and exploited the Negro race to the extent that Durkee has," Woodson announced.[45]

From 1920 until 1922, he served as a dean at West Virginia Collegiate Institute. In 1920, Woodson joined the Friends of Negro Freedom, a radical organization founded by Chandler Owens and A. Philip

Booker T. Washington. According to Woodson, Washington was "the greatest of all Americans." *Courtesy of West Virginia State Archives.*

Howard University's main building in Washington, D.C., circa 1900. *Courtesy of the Library of Congress.*

Randolph. While working at West Virginia Collegiate Institute, he also published his third major monograph, *The History of the Negro Church* (1921). Woodson advertised this study as the first serious historical study on the black church. He explored what he called "the greatest asset of the race" from the times when missionaries first converted blacks until the black church of the early twentieth century, underscoring that the black church and religion was a central cornerstone of black American culture.

In 1921, Woodson also wrote an unpublished manuscript, "The Case of the Negro." This document was rediscovered by historian Daryl Scott in 2005. Woodson's "lost-now-found" manuscript is an important document of early twentieth-century African American intellectual history as well as a revealing window into Woodson's radical thought and rhetoric. In this collection of essays, Woodson challenged the conventional racism of the times, called for drastic changes and reforms in the social order of American society, chastised white America for its collective mistreatment of blacks and critiqued black middle-class and elite leadership.

THE HISTORY OF THE
NEGRO CHURCH

BY

CARTER G. WOODSON, Ph.D.

*Editor of the Journal of Negro History, author of A Century of
Negro Migration, and of the Education of the Negro
Prior to 1861*

THE ASSOCIATED PUBLISHERS
WASHINGTON, D. C.

Labor and civil rights activist A. Philip Randolph. Woodson called Randolph a "twentieth-century prophet." *Courtesy of the Library of Congress.*

Opposite: The title page for *The History of the Negro Church* (1921). *Courtesy of the New York Public Library.*

That Woodson wrote "The Case of the Negro" and *The History of the Negro Church* in the same year speaks to his commitment to historical research. During the early 1920s, Woodson was busy with many other tasks. He was what we call today a "multitasker." He was directing the ASNLH, editing a journal and managing the Associated Publishers, Inc., which was incorporated in the District of Columbia on June 3, 1921. By 1923, the Associated Publishers, Inc., was used to identify the office-home that he purchased in July 1922. In 1923, Woodson had a sign eleven and a half feet wide and two feet high placed on the front façade of his home and the ASNLH headquarters to the right of the front door. The sign read in capital letters: "THE ASSOCIATED PUBLISHERS, INC." Woodson biographer Patricia W. Romero has provided an intriguing discussion of why Woodson decided to found the Associated Publishers, Inc. She concluded:

> *The Association had published some books prior to his establishing a publishing firm, but he had decided that the role of the Association should be distinguished from that of publisher. This was especially true in relation to outsiders wishing to publish through his organization. Rayford W. Logan…wrote that Woodson founded the Associated Publishers because Negro scholars encountered difficulty in publishing their works. There were, at that time, few places to which blacks could turn for publication, partly, said Logan, because few of them were trained scholars and partly because other publishers thought that they would not write objectively about themselves. According to Logan, Woodson believed that publishers of major firms did not think books written by Negroes, especially books of a scholarly nature, would sell to other blacks because they did not read volumes of this sort. Furthermore, it was thought whites and blacks were more interested in stories about Harlem dives than in scholarship. Woodson not only published the works of promising Negro historians, he also aided them financially at times so that they could spend time on research.*[46]

By 1922, Woodson decided to devote his life full time to the association. He resigned from his position at West Virginia Collegiate Institute and moved to Washington, D.C. On July 22, 1922, he purchased his office-home at 1538 Ninth Street, Northwest. For the next twenty-eight years, he devoted his life to maintaining the ASNLH and promoting black history. Woodson could have committed the lion's share of his work to

Woodson, when he was the dean at West Virginia Collegiate Institute, later West Virginia State College. *Courtesy of West Virginia State Archives.*

the academy. Lorenzo J. Greene thought that in the 1920s, Woodson "should be teaching at Harvard, Yale, Columbia, or some other ivy league school."[47] Woodson chose to fully dedicate and surrender his life to the study and promotion of black history instead.

In many respects the 1920s were "golden years" for the association. During this decade he received thousands of dollars from the Carnegie Foundation, the Julius Rosenwald Foundation and three Rockefeller trusts. These funds allowed him to hire young black scholars—including A.A. Taylor, Langston Hughes, Lorenzo J. Greene, Myra Colson Callis, Laura G. Glenn and Charles Wesley—to generate cutting edge scholarship. He also mentored many younger scholars. "Though he guarded his time like a soldier, he was always genuine with it when it came to 'young scholars,'" L.D. Reddick testified.[48] From 1922 until 1929, Woodson was prolific, publishing four articles in the *Journal of Negro History* and many books, including *Free Negro Owners of Slaves in the United States* (1924), *Free Negro Heads of Families in the United States in 1830* (1925), *Ten Years of Collecting and Publishing the Records of the Negro* (1925), *The Mind of the Negro as Reflected in Letters Written During the Crisis, 1800–1860* (1926), *Negro Orators and Their Orations* (1926*), *Negro Makers of History* (1928), *African Myths Together with Proverbs* (1928) and *The Negro as Businessman* (1929). Even though the association was rooted in black community infrastructures after its founding, by the mid-1920s, Woodson more actively strove to open the association's doors more widely to black people from various walks of life. By the early 1930s, after white philanthropists withdrew their support from the association, Woodson relied on black communities throughout the country, especially those in Washington D.C., to maintain the association's activities.

While the 1920s were prosperous times for the ASNLH because of the philanthropic funding it received, even during this decade Woodson made enormous sacrifices for the cause of black history. An interesting 1930 tribute to Woodson in the *Afro-American* shared with readers how instrumental Woodson was in maintaining the ASNLH during the 1920s:

> *The Association for the Study of Negro Life and History has been able to balance its annual budget of $20,000 because, as in former years, the Director, Carter G. Woodson, has served without compensation.*
>
> *Thousands of men and women have been able to take a neglected and despised cause like the chronicling of the history of a lowly people, and collection of ancient documents bearing upon such a chronicle, and*

Novelist Zora Neale Hurston was hired by Woodson and the ASNLH as a researcher in 1926. *Courtesy of the Library of Congress, Carl Van Vechten Collection.*

through the magic of sincerity, persistence and clear vision lift it to such a place of dignity and respect...

Our white folks lament that Negroes have never built a civilization, and men like Dr. Woodson rise up and point to the thick lips and kinky hair of the Sphinx...Dr. Woodson has worked without ceasing. His important book, "The Negro in Our History," which has gone through four editions, is probably more widely known among school children than any other single book...[T]eachers have been enlightened and inspired by Dr. Woodson, who in his lectures all over the country and by means of the annual meeting of the association, has educated the teachers as well as the public concerning the wide field of Negro history and the satisfying results which may be achieved by a thorough study.

The fact that the history association has not been able to pay Dr. Woodson a salary may be regarded as evidence of the public's failure to appreciate the services of the historian and the history association.

On the other hand, there are signs of increasing public regard for Dr. Woodson, and his contributions to history, and well might there be.

He has blazed a new trail. He has put old truths to a new light. He has brought a new light to those who sat in darkness. He has made it possible for every Negro lad to hold his head a little higher and set his chin a little firmer.

He has made it possible for a race to face the future with greater hope because he has taken the cover off the past.

Two or three more men like Dr. Woodson and even inaccurate news magazines like "Time" will cease claiming the Egyptians and the Abyssinians for the white race.[49]

One of Woodson's most important contributions to the early black history movement was his mission and ability to transform black history into a practical and popular medium for uplifting blacks and challenging racial prejudice. In adopting this approach, he did not deemphasize the role of rigorous scholarship in the "life-and-death struggle" for black liberation. On the other hand, he maintained that in addition to being founded on rigorous research, the study and dissemination of black history should extend to the working-class and youthful sectors of the black community. Woodson reasoned that the knowledge of African American history could psychologically empower black people. Between 1915 and 1950, he strove to enlighten the black masses, popularizing black history in a variety of ways.

Woodson in 1930. *Scurlock Studio Records, ca. 1905–1994, Archives Center, National Museum of American History, Smithsonian Institution.*

Woodson's practical approach to using black history as a tool of psychological empowerment and liberation was heightened by his pessimistic view of American politics. "Throughout the 1930s and 1940s Woodson continued his advocacy of black political independence and retained no ties to any party."[50] In September 1932, on the eve of the 1932

African American youth selling copies of the *Chicago Defender* in 1942. During the 1930s and 1940s, Woodson published numerous essays in this leading black newspaper. *Courtesy of the Library of Congress.*

U.S. presidential election, Woodson declared: "So far as the two major parties are concerned, we cannot expect any benefit from either. These parties are not trying to help humanity. They are merely using humanity as a means to selfish ends."[51] In another essay, Woodson revealed his distrust in politicians: "The New Negro in politics is not a politician. He is a man. He is not trying to give the world something rather than extract something from it…If he goes into office it will be as a sacrifice, because his valuable time is required elsewhere."[52]

Woodson's most famous and perhaps most effective effort at attracting a mass following and popularizing the study of black history was through Negro History Week celebrations. But before 1926, when he inaugurated this celebration, Woodson took black history to the people in other ways. Between the founding of the ASNLH and his death, Woodson and his entourage spoke at various venues. According to an editorial in the *Chicago Defender*, Woodson educated "hundreds of thousands of students in thousands of schools all over the world." Students appreciated his contributions. On February 16, 1946, the *Washington Post* reported in an editorial, "Students Honor Carter Woodson," that students from the Charles Young School paid homage to Woodson by presenting him with a "scroll containing the names of 1080 pupils" and by reenacting his life story in a play.

Woodson corresponded with countless people from all around the world interested in black history. He answered their questions, commented on papers and mailed them information pertaining to black history. Since the organization's inception, Woodson commented in *Ten Years of Collecting and Publishing the Records of the Negro*, the ASNLH had functioned as a "free reference bureau" regarding the study of black life and history. Before Negro History Week, Woodson also attempted to stir interest in black history among the youth with financial incentives. In 1924, for instance, in collaboration with the American Folklore Society, the association offered a $200 prize "for the best collection of tales, riddles, proverbs, sayings, and songs, which have been heard at home by Negro students of accredited schools."[53] In 1927, a year after the founding of Negro History Week, Woodson established the Association's Extension Division in order to expose more people to black history through public lectures and correspondence study. Besides Negro History Week, another form of major extension work undertaken by the association director was the *Negro History Bulletin*, an easy-to-read black history magazine.

While the 1920s were arguably the association's "golden years" in financial terms, the 1930s and the 1940s were challenging. "After 1933 no white foundation made substantial contribution to the association, and Woodson was forced to depend almost totally on the black community for the financial support necessary to continue his campaign to promote Negro history."[54] In a letter to Arthur Spingarn dated June 13, 1936, Woodson observed: "Few whites now help because we are too independent."[55] During the economically stifling 1930s and 1940s, Woodson opted for independence. "Rather than give up his autonomy,

Woodson preferred to struggle financially. Indeed, the 1930s would prove to be a struggle," historian Jacqueline Goggin surmised. She continued:

> *Yet, these financial challenges were met by economizing, increasing administrative efficiency, and planning creatively. At the same time, Woodson further extended his reach to the masses of black Americans, and in doing so, broadened the base of his movement and heightened the black community's racial pride and cultural consciousness. To ease his physical and mental stress during the troublesome depression decade, he spent several summers in Europe, taking extended vacations for the first time in his life.*[56]

During the 1930s and 1940s, the association struggled to break even at the end of each fiscal year. By 1949, Woodson had borrowed several thousand dollars to maintain the association and in his final 1949 annual review, he lamented:

> *Problems have arisen, but the management with the cooperation of warm friends of the effort have contrived to solve most of them. The chief difficulty is the disparity between the increase and expenditures of the organization. While its income remains about the same the cost of operating is about seventy per cent more than it was a few years ago. It was necessary, therefore, for the Association to borrow two thousand dollars to meet pressing obligations. In the meantime the management will make a special effort to increase the income to the level of expenditure.*[57]

From 1915 until his death, Woodson's "bride was truly the Association and to her he left his worldly goods and his files. It was found after his death that the Association owed him a considerable amount in salary which he had never seen fit to collect. The Association needed it more."[58] The association was, as Woodson put it, "my offspring," "my intellectual child." A month following Woodson's death, John Hope Franklin noted that after founding the association, "for the next thirty-five years he [Woodson] was to labor unceasingly in the task of reconstructing the history of a people and of rehabilitating their place in society on the basis of that history. Few men in any generation have worked so tirelessly and effectively toward their chosen goal."[59] "At the peak of his career as an educator," ASNLH activist Albert N.D. Brooks told students who filled an auditorium at Carter G. Woodson Junior High School in Washington,

D.C., in 1956, "Woodson turned his back on high-salaried positions to devote his life to a cause."[60] From 1915 until 1950, Woodson's name was synonymous with "Negro history" and the ASNLH.

Woodson died suddenly from a heart attack on April 3, 1950. The *Pittsburgh Courier* (Washington edition) published the following about Woodson's death:

> *Woodson was found dead by friends who forced entry into his residence at 1538 Ninth Street, NW, shortly after noon Monday. He was pronounced dead by his physician, Howard University professor Dr. Henry A. Callis, who conjectured that the eminent scholar died peacefully, while in bed. Mrs. Jessie Robinson, office manager of the Associated Publishers, Inc., the venture founded by Dr. Woodson in 1922, told* The Courier *that she heard him stirring in his quarters, located on the third floor of the office building, earlier in the day and that he had evidently retired again. He had been suffering from a heart ailment for the past several years, she disclosed, but she did not become uneasy until he failed to "come down to the office" at 12:30 as usual. Mrs. Robinson called a personal friend of the nationally known man, Arnett G. Lindsay, and asked him to investigate. Mr. Lindsay forced the door, after repeated knocking brought no response and found Dr. Woodson lying in bed. Noting the coldness of his hands, and detecting no heartbeat, he summoned the office staff and asked that Dr. Callis be summoned.*[61]

The *Call: Southwest's Leading Weekly* added that Woodson "was found dead in his bed in his apartment about 2 o'clock in the afternoon by Arnett G. Lindsay" and that Woodson "had been up the night before until 11 o'clock talking to friends."[62] In a letter to the editor of the *Washington Post* on April 8, 1950, Woodson's physician, Henry Arthur Callis, requested that Woodson's death be recognized like that of Charles Drew, and he offered another explanation for the cause of the ASNLH founder's death. "The immediate cause of Dr. Woodson's death was the shock of the loss of Charles R. Drew," Callis concluded.[63] The association founder's sudden death shocked his co-workers.

Immediately following Woodson's funeral services at Shiloh Baptist Church in Washington, D.C., the association's executive council and many of Woodson's "Boys" met at the association headquarters at 1538 Ninth Street, Northwest, "to decide whether the Association would continue." The meeting was called by Woodson's logical successor, Charles H.

A painting of physician, surgeon and medical researcher Charles R. Drew by Betsy Graves Reyneau. A native of Washington, D.C., Drew died one week before Woodson. *Courtesy of the National Archives and Records Administration.*

Wesley. Woodson's associates realized that their deceased leader truly *was* the association; it was "his own private preserve" and "his creation."[64] Acting Secretary Arnett G. Lindsay was honored by Wesley's proposal that he serve as the managing editor of the *Journal of Negro History* and the *Negro History Bulletin*, "but was of the opinion, since Woodson's work was at least four-fold that the continuation of the Association's program would have to be divided among four or five interested members."[65]

In his first "Report of the Director" in October 1950, Rayford W. Logan reiterated Lindsay: "It would be impossible for any one to carry out the multitudinous tasks that Dr. Woodson had learned, through the years, to perform with efficiency and dispatch."[66] In retrospect, Woodson perhaps did not adequately prepare the organization for the future. For instance, when he was asked at the association's annual meeting in Columbus, Ohio, in 1945 about sharing the leadership responsibilities of the association with his "Boys," he reminded them that "the Association was his creation. He had built it, sacrificed for it, and he would continue to direct it until his death."[67] According to a 1950 article in the *Chicago Defender*, "Set 1st History Meet Since Woodson's Death," association officials believed that "it will be necessary to refashion the body's entire structure in order to keep it going and meet the increasing demands for its services. There is much talk of 'clearing out old timber' and 'injecting new blood' into the governing board."[68]

As L.D. Reddick surmised, though Woodson "noticeably mellowed" in "the last year of his life" and "appeared to be trying to learn to delegate important tasks, to let others lift some of the load from his individual shoulders," during the early 1950s, the association failed to

> *make the transition smoothly...principally because no one has been found as yet who can afford or will afford to run the risk of making the work of the Association his full-time job. Many capable and willing hands will help with this or that part-time duty but the Association requires a full-time director. What a wonderful opportunity for some young scholar! What a great chance to continue the work of a truly great man! What a strategic moment in history to help American culture become more democratic!*[69]

At the closing session of the ASNLH annual meeting in Nashville, Tennessee, on October 25, 1953, Wesley echoed Reddick, calling on the association to return to its status of being a "servant" to "a number of publics" and to continue to popularize black history as Woodson strove to.

2

WOODSON AND THE EARLY BLACK HISTORY MOVEMENT IN THE NATION'S CAPITAL

Most honorable mention, however, belongs to Washington, D.C., where without any urgent solicitation from $1,500 to $2,000 is annually raised to support the work of the Association. The Shaw Junior School, about two blocks from the national office in Washington, raises more money for the cause than any other school in the world...Just as the Shaw Junior High School takes priority among the schools so does the Helping Hand Club of the Nineteenth Street Baptist Church take priority of the country. This city-wide interchurch is in a class by itself...It stages annually drives to aid...the Association for the Study of Negro Life and History...In this connection should be mentioned the large number of teachers of the District of Columbia who, although prohibited by local regulations from receiving solicitors in the school, voluntarily connect themselves as members of the Association and subscribers to its magazines.
—*Carter G. Woodson, 1947*[70]

Woodson's decision to establish the ASNLH's headquarters at 1538 Ninth Street, Northwest, in Washington, D.C., is not surprising. Not only was the city the nation's capital located—as Woodson observed in 1917—"mid-way between the North and the South," but during the Progressive era, Washington, D.C., "became a black intellectual and civil rights capital."[71] Numerous prominent Washington, D.C. African American businesses, educators, churches and leaders supported Woodson's early black history movement, especially during annual Negro History Week celebrations and the association's nine annual meetings in the nation's capital between 1917 and 1949. Washington, D.C., was home to Howard University, numerous national archives and the Library of Congress. Between 1929 and 1938, Woodson established a documentary trove on African American history at the Library of Congress, what is now called the Carter Godwin Woodson Papers.

According to the 1920 U.S. census, there were more than 110,000 African Americans residing in Washington, D.C., representing approximately 25 percent of the city's total population. Only New York City and Chicago had larger black populations. The area where Woodson decided to settle down was in 1966 dubbed by many as *Shaw*, derived from the name of a popular D.C. public junior high school, and referred to the area "bounded by North Capital an[d] 15th streets, NW, on the east and west and Florida Avenue and M Street, NW, on the north and south."[72] From "the boisterous 1920s to the riots of the 1960s, the area north of downtown Washington known today as 'Shaw' was the pre-eminent African American neighborhood in the city."[73] Also known as "Washington's Harlem," Shaw, "despite acknowledged divisions based on color and class, functioned well for its members. Shaw was a dense weave of personal acquaintances and lifelong friendships based in strong families, churches, schools, fraternal and social clubs, black-owned businesses, and other local institutions. These provided support, training, and opportunities for important individual and group achievements," Kathryn S. Smith has posited. "What the residents of Shaw created under segregation—faced with a larger society that refused them dignity and opportunity—was a place to act and decide. It was a place where they could shape their own lives. Racial segregation was the outside agent forcing these residents to build a separate community."[74] As suggested by Michele F. Pacifico, the neighborhood boasted "more vocal leaders and highly trained and educated African Americans than most other American cities. Because of their proximity to national power, educated black Washingtonians considered themselves national figures as well as local leaders."[75] More recently, historian Zachery Williams has argued that during the early twentieth century, the nation's capital fostered the development of a dynamic black intellectual community that rivaled the Harlem Renaissance.

There were certainly economically deprived blacks living in the vicinity of Woodson's office-home. Yet "Black Broadway" was significantly different from where Washington, D.C.'s struggling and poor blacks lived. During the 1920s, the population whom William Henry Jones called Washington, D.C.'s "Negro city dwellers" constituted a diverse group who lived "all over Washington" but disproportionately inhabited the city's alleys.[76] There were many challenges facing blacks in D.C. around the time that Woodson settled there. For example, it was not until 1919—the same year that a race riot engulfed the city in July and that John Whitelaw Lewis opened the first hotel and apartment building for African Americans—"that Washington's black birthrate began to exceed the population's mortality rate."[77] As historian Elizabeth Clark-Lewis has underscored, the vast majority of the city's working black women labored as domestic servants. Woodson himself noted the vast discrepancy in the progress made by the "highly educated persons of the District of Columbia" compared with the city's black "masses" between 1880 and 1931. Sympathetic to the "masses" of his people, he did on rare occasions publicly echo the civilizationist sentiments of Washington D.C.'s black bourgeoisie. "For some time I have been making a special study in Washington, and I try to compare our condition of today with that of the past. Now although the few highly educated persons of the District of Columbia have multiplied and are in better circumstances than ever, the masses show almost as much backwardness as they did in 1880," Woodson observed in 1931. "Although born and brought up in the Black Belt of the South, I never saw there such idolatrous tendencies as I have seen under the dome of the Capitol." At the same time, Woodson in part blamed D.C.'s "highly educated," himself included, for abandoning what he termed the "undeveloped man."[78] According to the *Pittsburgh Courier*, during a lecture in Camden, New Jersey, in 1934 Woodson said, "There are more fool Negroes to the square inch in Washington, D.C., than any other city."[79]

When Woodson opened the doors of the association and the Associated Publishers, Inc., black businesses in Washington, D.C. were making significant progress. Though the evolution of independent black businesses in D.C. was profoundly shaped by the efforts of a range of leaders during the Progressive era—such as William Calvin Chase, John Wesley Cromwell, Alexander Crummell, Edward E. Cooper, William H. Davis, Andrew Hilyer and the "Four Hundred of Washington"—in the mid-1880s, there were only fifteen black businesses operating in the Shaw area. Yet "by 1920 there were well over 300."[80] Equally important, there was also a concrete tradition of black historical organizations in Washington, D.C., before the association secured a permanent home there, including the Bethel Literary and Historical Association (founded in 1881), the Garnett Literary Association (founded in 1890), the American Negro Academy (founded

An African American family pose outside their home in one of the "alley dwelling" sections of Washington, D.C., in 1943. *Courtesy of the Library of Congress.*

The Whitelaw Hotel, the first hotel and apartment building for African Americans in Washington, D.C., was opened by John Whitelaw Lewis. During several of the ASNLH's annual meetings in Washington, D.C., the Whitelaw Hotel was used for sessions and lodging. *Courtesy of the Library of Congress.*

The office of the *Washington Bee*, Washington, D.C., in 1899. *Courtesy of the Library of Congress.*

in 1897), the Frederick Douglass Memorial and Historical Association (founded in 1900), the Washington Conservatory of Music (founded in 1905) and the Mu-So-Lit Club. Founded in the same year as the ASNLH, the Mu-So-Lit Club preceded its counterpart in holding an annual black history celebration during February in honor of Frederick Douglass's and Abraham Lincoln's birthdays. Its members also worked hand in hand with the association, hosting at its 1327 R Street, Northwest, headquarters several of the sessions for the ASNLH annual meeting in 1929. Still, the ASNLH was larger and was also the only organization of its kind to establish concrete and enduring programs for D.C.'s black public school children.

From 1922 until his death, Woodson consciously chose to live in Washington, D.C. It is not unreasonable to deduce that he must have liked the District of Columbia. Before committing his life's work to the ASNLH in 1922, he worked at several different D.C. black high schools and at Howard University and frequented the desegregated Library of Congress. In summarizing the events of the ASNLH's "First Biennial Meeting," Woodson highlighted the importance of Washington, D.C., as a base of operations for the ASNLH and how his organization contributed to the city's progressive black culture. "There is no fixed rule to determine exactly where the meetings of the Association shall be held," Woodson noted. He went on to say:

Washington, however, naturally proved attractive for the reasons that it is located mid-way between the North and the South, the Association is incorporated under laws of the District of Columbia, and several of its officers reside there. The extensive advertising given the meeting and the occurrence of the conference in Washington on the education of the Negro the following day brought to the meeting probably the largest number of useful and scholarly Negroes ever assembled at the national capital.[81]

At the same time, the city that Woodson noted as being located "mid-way between the North and the South" exhibited many of the characteristics of the Jim Crow South. There was rampant racial discrimination in the District of Columbia during the era of Jim Crow segregation, and as late as 1953, when Dwight D. Eisenhower became president, the city was elaborately segregated. The following description of segregation, Washington, D.C. style, from chairman of the Publicity Committee for the Coordinating Committee for the Enforcement of the D.C. Anti-Discrimination Laws Marvin Caplan concisely summarizes the realities faced by the national capital's black population:

By 1950, segregation by law and by custom was firmly entrenched in Washington. Segregated restaurants were only one reflection of a racially divided city. Black Washingtonians encountered segregation in the most fundamental aspects of their daily lives. Housing and public schools were segregated. Only one hospital, Freedman's, admitted blacks without segregation, and several would not admit black patients at all. While the federal government offered some opportunities for skilled employment, blacks, in the main, were relegated to perform the capital's menial tasks—as its messengers, porters, day laborers and domestics. Blacks who ventured downtown found most hotels and movie houses closed to them. The National Theatre, Washington's one legitimate playhouse, excluded blacks, a policy that so incensed the Actors' Equity Association that it instituted a boycott against the place. Most recreation facilities, public and private, were segregated as well. Glen Echo, the area's one amusement park, was closed to blacks, a restriction that left countless black youngsters heartbroken.[82]

In her classic study on the "secret city," Constance Green highlighted that "except for the haunts of bootleggers and other elements of the underworld" and "on the trolleys and buses, at Griffith Stadium, and in the readings rooms of the public library and the Library of Congress,"[83] by 1923 racial segregation persisted everywhere in Washington, D.C. Shortly after Woodson purchased his office-home, racism in the nation's capital was epitomized on August 8, 1925, when more than thirty thousand members of the Ku Klux Klan marched in full regalia down Pennsylvania Avenue.

In Washington, D.C., Woodson embarked on his career as a scholar-activist. He was active in secondary education, a known and controversial figure on Howard University's campus and belonged to a range of organizations including the Committee of 200, the National Urban League, the Washington branch of the NAACP, the New Negro Alliance and the Committee of 50. In June 1922, Woodson "participated in the Washington [NAACP] branch's silent march against lynching."[84] During the 1930s and 1940s, Woodson also critiqued the racial inequalities that blacks endured in the nation's capital in many of his newspaper columns. He was concerned with the plight of the unemployed black masses in D.C. as exemplified in the Associated Publishers, Inc.'s *Employment of Negroes in the District of Columbia* (1931) and his presentation before the Federation of Civic Associations at the District Building in March 1932. One *Washington Post* writer noted that Woodson "discussed the color line as it exists in Washington industry, showing changes in employment of Negro workers during recent years, steps taken toward opening new avenues of employment, and the effects of organization of Negro labor. Special consideration was given the trend of employment by the National Government unfavorable to the Negro in the departmental service."[85]

Woodson also directly challenged racism in D.C. that impacted him in more direct and personal ways. In December 1932, he boldly indicted the Chesapeake and Ohio Railroad office in Washington, D.C., after being denied Pullman accommodations on November 26, 1932. His letter of protest was printed in at least one black newspaper:

This is merely to say that the Ku Klux Klan policy still dominates your City Ticket Office at 1714 14ʰ Street, N.W., Washington, D.C. The management there still refuses to sell Negroes reservations except when they have Lower 1 available; and some of the clerks do not want to sell that. I have written to you to this effect several times, and no change in this policy has been noted. The management here in Washington, however, had rather see the road go into the hands of a receiver than sell a Negro a Pullman berth. This may be a fine way to promote the

Ku Klux Klan movement, but it will never do for running a business. Inasmuch as this is your policy, I am going to West Virginia by another route which does not champion the cause of the Ku Klux Klan...The only thing we can do, then, is to advise self-respecting Negroes to travel on some other road whenever they can.[86]

Woodson was a recognized community man of the Shaw neighborhood who routinely traveled through the city by foot. Woodson "never bought a car for himself in order to exercise by walking." He walked "whenever possible, whether to church, the Post Office, Library of Congress, or to the home where he ate dinner, no matter how inclement the weather."[87] Based on his educational achievements, Woodson was undoubtedly a member of D.C.'s "highly-educated" class of blacks that he so often berated. Nevertheless, probably influenced by his poor, working-class background, he deliberately rejected many of the cultural mores, values and behavioral patterns of the majority of D.C.'s black elite. He could have owned a car or relied on public transportation. Instead, he more often than not opted to move around D.C. by foot. This certainly provided him with an intimate view of city life. Woodson viewed blacks who drove expensive cars as victims of what Norwegian American sociologist and economist Thornstein Veblen described as "conspicuous consumption" in *The Theory of the Leisure Class* (1899). "The other day I was accosted by a young woman driving an expensive car," Woodson recounted during the peak of the Great Depression. "She wanted to give me a lift, but I was not going exactly in her direction. I feel uncomfortable anyway when associating with people of this type, for I cannot return these favors while earning about twelve and a half dollars a week and serving as caretaker in our building in return for free use of the attic in order to save rent."[88]

Yet one evening, Woodson discovered the dangers of walking on D.C. streets at night. On June 13, 1933, he was robbed at gunpoint by "two colored thugs." Woodson shared his experiences with *Chicago Defender*, *Pittsburgh Courier*, *Afro-American* and *New York Amsterdam News* readers in detail and with some humor:

In the evening of the unlucky Friday, the thirteenth of this month, I had my superstition confirmed beyond the shadow of a doubt. Going from the Library of Congress toward Pennsylvania, I had an unusual experience just before I reached Peace Monument which temporarily became a scene of war. Two colored thugs rushed upon me from the rear, caught me by both of my hands, stuck a gun in my side, struck me on one cheek because I came near disengaging myself from them; and, before I could religiously turn the other cheek, gave me a stunning blow on the other side of my head. Seeing what I was facing, I begged them not to kill me and offered them what money I had. After dispossessing me of five dollars they ran away.

This was the first time in my life that I have had any one to pay me the compliment of having money. While I regret the loss of my money and cannot enjoy the sore head and black eye, I had the chance to learn some of the things which we read about in books or see in the movies. The experience, too, was very illuminating; and if you have never had it you have something to look forward to.[89]

Despite his experiences, Woodson defended and sympathized with impoverished African American men in D.C. who chose a life of crime. "So many poor people of our group have little to do now except gambling, racketeering, and stealing. They are hungry, and they are going to kill and rob before they settle down to starvation." Woodson added that he sought to "remedy" this situation in the District of Columbia by "petitioning employers of labor to provide in some way for the large number of our unemployed" and by encouraging the growth of black businesses.[90]

Woodson routinely dined at the Phyllis Wheatley YWCA at 901 Rhode Island Avenue that was half a block north of his office-home and regularly hosted sessions for the ASNLH's annual meetings in D.C. After his ritual meal, he would "often linger afterwards in the lobby, sitting and chatting with the young ladies who resided there."[91] He also dined at the Gateway Dining Room in Union Station. The female residents of the Phyllis Wheatley YWCA were especially fond of Woodson.

Many evenings when he dropped in for dinner in the Y.W.C.A. dining room, Dr. Woodson would casually linger in the comfortable Lobby late into the evening. Seated there like the great philosopher and teacher that he was, he would engage in stimulating conversations with the young women as they passed, tarried and listened to learn from experiences of his full rich life. He was a fountainhead of knowledge of our history and racial heritage, together with an interesting store of anecdotes of wit and humor. There were also periods of healthy philosophy, wise counsel, and current information. His wide travel experience as teacher, lecturer, instructor, leader, and humanitarian

The Phillis Wheatley YWCA located at 901 Rhode Island Avenue, Northwest, in the Shaw neighborhood of Washington, D.C. Woodson used to eat there and talk with the residents. *Courtesy of Wikimedia Commons.*

made him always welcome as an interesting and entertaining visitor. As a conversationalist he would, when pressed, modestly relate marvelous incidents of his own early life. His optimistic views and worthwhile topics were impelling and contagious.[92]

Many who chipped past his rugged exterior said that there was a soft spot for children in his heart. Below several rare photos of Woodson under the heading "'Schoolmaster to His Race' Mourned" in the *Afro-American* (Washington), there is a caption stating: "Above are typical pictures of the late Dr. Woodson who died suddenly, Monday. Creator of Negro History Week, celebrated throughout the nation, Dr. Woodson was never happier than when surrounded by children who idolized him."[93] The children who lived near Woodson's office-home appreciated him. He shared historical stories and African folktales with them and "enjoyed taking little treats of candy to the neighborhood children around 9th Street, or buying them ice cream."[94] During Negro History Week in 1932, a *Washington Post* editorial publicized Woodson's hands-on interaction with D.C.'s African American youth:

Congressman Oscar DePriest. Woodson supported his election to the House of Representatives, and DePriest supported Negro History Week celebrations in Washington, D.C. *Courtesy of the Library of Congress.*

Now known as Ashbury Dwellings, this building used to be Shaw Junior High School. *Courtesy of Wikimedia Commons.*

Approximately 1,000 colored school children gathered yesterday in the caucus room in the House Office Building in connection with the annual celebration of Negro history week, sponsored by the Association for the Study of Negro Life and History, Dr. Carter G. Woodson, director, to meet Representative Oscar DePriest, of Illinois. Other members of Congress who witnessed the exercises were Representative Henry T. Rainey and Representative W.E. Hull, of Illinois; Representative U.S. Guyer, of Kansas, and Representative Frank Murphy, of Ohio.[95]

While cities like Chicago, New York, Detroit, Los Angeles and Atlanta were known for having successful annual Negro History Week celebrations, those in Washington, D.C., were especially successful. During the ASNLH's first thirty-five years, Howard University hosted more than a few sessions of the annual ASNLH meetings as well as Negro History Week celebrations. At the association's annual meeting in 1937, for instance, participants visited Howard University's Gallery of Art to see the work of Henry Ossawa Tanner and enjoyed performances from Howard's Glee Club under the direction of Professor Roy W. Tibbs. Among the most active Howard University professors in the association and D.C.'s early black history movement were Charles H. Wesley, Alain L. Locke, Benjamin Brawley, Lois M. Jones, Dorothy Burnett, James A. Porter, Eva B. Dykes, W. Montague Cobb, Marion Thompson Wright and Sterling Brown. Woodson praised black Washingtonians, often teachers and schoolchildren, for leading the way in popularizing black history. In 1942, Woodson summarized the creative efforts—including "show-and-tell" exercises and a hands-on assembly—of "the pupils of the 4B Grade of the Morse School in Washington, D.C."[96] In April 1947, Woodson extolled blacks in Washington, D.C., especially those in the Shaw neighborhood connected to Shaw Junior High School, for raising "more money for the cause than any other school in the world."[97] In 1949, Woodson shared with *Negro History Bulletin* readers how numerous Washington, D.C. schoolteachers helped him with the annual Negro History Week pamphlet.[98] Other African American schools in the nation's capital that were active in the early black history movement included Garrett-Patterson High School, Dunbar High School, Cardozo Business School, Randall Junior High School, Frazier Junior High School, Miner Normal College, Armstrong Training School, Banneker Junior High School, and Nannie Helen Burrough's National Training School for Women and Girls.

WOODSON'S CHURCH AFFILIATIONS
IN WASHINGTON, D.C.

The day before Woodson's funeral, friends "were invited to call at the McGuire Funeral Home, 1820 9th st. n.w.," a black-owned funeral home founded in 1912. The funeral services were held at 1:00 p.m. on April 8, 1950, at the Shiloh Baptist Church, at 1500 Ninth Street, Northwest, and the Reverend Earl L. Harrison, Shiloh's fourth pastor from 1930 until 1971, "conducted the impressive rites" and delivered a scripture reading. Several ministers—including Woodson's close friend Dr. Jerry Moore, pastor of the Nineteenth Street Baptist Church; Reverend W.H. Jernagin, pastor of Mt. Carmel Baptist Church; and Reverend R.R. Brooks, pastor of the Lincoln Congregational Church—delivered brief tributes and prayers in his honor. "Madame Lillian Evanti, famed soprano, sang a spiritual and 'The 23rd Psalm.' The congregation joined in the singing of two hymns, 'Majestic Sweetness Sits Enthroned' and 'His Eyes Is on the Sparrow.'"[99] The interment was in Lincoln Cemetery, a cemetery in Prince George County, Maryland, founded in 1927 for the African American community.

Woodson did not write extensively about his relationship with or views of Shiloh Baptist Church. In 1935, in response to charges that he told three thousand black Detroiters "jammed [in] the large gymnasium" in the YMCA to "scrap all religion," he briefly discussed his church participation. "I am a member of a church myself and recently when attending contributed ten dollars to its support. I am wondering how one thus associated and functioning can be in favor of destroying the church," Woodson retorted. "In all my writings, moreover, I have tried to make it clear that the Negro church is about the only thing that the Race has developed in America."[100] While it does not appear that Shiloh was used extensively for the association's functions during the first three meetings held in D.C. between 1917 and 1920, the last major session for the annual ASNLH meeting in 1942 in the nation's capital was held at Shiloh Baptist Church and most of the sessions for the 1948 ASNLH annual meeting were held there. In 1948, Reverend Earl L. Harrison also delivered the welcoming address for the conference. Shiloh Baptist Church was especially active in Negro History Week celebrations during the 1940s. The Negro History Week celebration in 1946 in Washington, D.C., for instance, was "more widely observed...than ever" and one of the most successful events was "the well attended and highly successful

Negro History Week Dinner annually given by the Shiloh Baptist Church, Dr. E.L. Harrison, pastor."[101]

In Woodson's mind, the church was an important element of African American culture. He acknowledged the central place of the black church in African American culture in *The History of the Negro Church* (1921), he held large annual ASNLH functions in black churches throughout D.C. and the nation and he delivered talks and lectures in numerous black churches in the capital and the country. On one occasion, Woodson spoke at a Baptist church in Washington, D.C., "to make an appeal in behalf of Miss Nannie H. Burroughs's school."[102] Though Woodson critiqued ministers, church pastors played important roles in annual meetings, and religion was discussed at more than a few sessions. At the ASNLH's tenth-anniversary meeting in Washington, D.C., in 1925, for instance, there was a session devoted to the black church that was briefly reviewed in the *Washington Post* on September 6, 1925. Churches were pivotal in many of the Negro History Week celebrations in Washington, D.C. On February 9, 1931, a reporter for the *Washington Post* remarked that Negro History Week services were held "in all colored churches here and in adjacent communities." Similarly, in 1945, a writer for the *Negro History Bulletin* attested that in the nation's capital "the churches especially became active. The climax in the National Capital was the meeting of the Helping Hand Club, under the inspiration of Mrs. E.C. Bannister, at the Nineteenth Baptist Church where addresses were delivered by Dr. Charlotte Hawkins Brown and Congresswoman Helen Gehagan Douglas."[103]

Woodson was also a member of Nineteenth Street Baptist Church's nondenominational Helping Hand Club. Dubbed by John W. Cromwell the first Baptist church "among the Negroes of the District of Columbia," Nineteenth Baptist Church was founded on August 29, 1839, by Sampson White and remained on the corner of Nineteenth and I Streets, Northwest, in D.C. until it moved to its current location at 4606 Sixteenth Street, Northwest, in January 1975. Since 1839, the church has had thirteen pastors. During Woodson's lifetime, two pastors served: Dr. Walter Henderson Brooks and Dr. Jerry A. Moore Jr. Under the leadership of Brooks, a prominent member of the ASNLH, the Nineteenth Street Baptist Church flourished and exhibited progressive gender politics. Not only did Brooks mentor and support women like Jennie Deane, founder of the Manassas Industrial School in Virginia, and Nannie Helen Burroughs, but on July 21, 1896, the National Association of Colored Women was organized in Brooks's church with

Nineteenth Street Baptist Church, Washington, D.C. Woodson was a member of this church's Helping Hand Club. *Courtesy of the Library of Congress.*

Washingtonian Mary Church Terrell being elected as the organization's first president.

Woodson did not talk a great deal about being a member of Nineteenth Street Baptist Church's Helping Hand Club, but he praised Brooks and the church's outreach work. "Probably no man living has exemplified actual Christian living better than [Brooks] who now at the age of ninety-four is still active in the service of the Master," Woodson proclaimed in 1946.[104] Woodson also praised other members and activities of Nineteenth Street Baptist Church, especially the Helping Hand Club during the leadership of Jerry A. Moore Jr. In 1949, the Associated Publishers, Inc., published *History of the Helping Hand Club of the Nineteenth Baptist Street Church.* Woodson's description of this church's uplift organization sheds some light on his own religious philosophy:

> *This city-wide interchurch organization is in a class by itself. Although organized in a Baptist Church, its members consist of persons of all faith. They cooperate in helping the poor and the afflicted and give aid to causes projected for the good of humanity. Mrs. Ella C. Bannister, a woman of high ideals and Christian influence in the city, is the president of this club. It stages annually drives to aid the National Association for the Advancement of Colored People and for the Association for the Study of Negro Life and History. At a mass meeting in the city on the 14th of February the club raised more than $400 for the Association, and workers are weekly reporting other amounts which will increase the sum to $500.[105]*

AN APPRECIATED HOME WITH MULTIPLE FUNCTIONS

Built sometime between about 1872 and 1874 (the specific architect(s) and builders(s) is/are unknown at this time), the three-story, Victorian-style brick row house Woodson purchased from agents George F. Cook and A.W. Mitchell on July 18, 1922, on Lot 819 in Square 365 at 1538 Ninth Street, Northwest, was $8,000. Woodson's acquisition of a home in D.C. was not a unique phenomenon for African Americans in D.C. during the 1920s. According to sociologist William Henry Jones, during the decade, "it was not unusual to encounter cases of Negro families which have purchased homes on a cash basis for $10,000 to $25,000... The purchase price of the average home that is acquired by Negroes is between $6,000 and $7,000."[106] On the eve of purchasing the home at 1538 Ninth Street, Northwest, Woodson rented office space for the ASNLH on U Street. Eight months before purchasing his new home,

Woodson and the association listed "1216 You Street, NW, Washington, D.C.," as its headquarters and mailing address. From the founding of the association until 1919, Woodson used his apartment at 2223 Twelfth Street, Northwest, as his organization's base of operations. Woodson did not celebrate or even announce the acquisition of his new 1538 Ninth Street, Northwest home in the "Notes" or "Director's Report" sections or

Woodson in 1925, several years after he devoted himself full time
to the ASNLH. *Scurlock Studio Records, ca. 1905–1994, Archives Center,
National Museum of American History, Smithsonian Institution.*

Opposite: Woodson's office-home and the headquarters of the
ASNLH and the Associated Publishers, Inc., 1538 Ninth Street,
Northwest, Washington, DC. *Used with permission from the Afro-American
Newspapers Archives and Research Center.*

anywhere else in the *Journal of Negro History*. The first publically published
listing of this new address for the ASNLH headquarters in the *Journal*
was in July 1923.

With a capital stock of $25,000, the Associated Publishers, Inc., offered
black and white professionally trained scholars as well as black female
schoolteachers and race reformers the opportunity to publish "all kinds

of information concerning the Negro race and those who have been interested in its uplift," Woodson announced in the summer of 1921.[107] A decade after founding the Associated Publishers, Inc., Woodson explained the mission of the ASNLH's publishing firm. "We have no desire to make money," Woodson asserted. "We seek merely to serve humanity."[108] After chastising mainstream white university "publishing houses," including those at Yale, Columbia and Johns Hopkins, Woodson stressed the importance of the Associated Publishers, Inc.:

> *In the case of the Associated Publishers in Washington, D.C, they have such an establishment which has thus functioned for ten years. Such a publishing house, moreover, renders a much higher service than a purely commercial one. It evaluates the productions presented to it not on the basis of what others may think about them but on the basis of their value in the promotion of the truth. It supplies schools and libraries with valuable information not only as to what this firm has produced but makes the effort to supply the particular needs of institutions. This house undertakes to point out and to assist in securing the most valuable books bearing upon the Negro whether published in this country or abroad.[109]*

The Associated Publishers, Inc., was one of the few commercial black book publishing companies active during the era of Jim Crow segregation, and the business was largely Woodson's. He "owned 95 percent of the stock in the Associated Publishers and paid his salary from its profits."[110] Though in financial terms, the Associated Publishers, Inc., did not reap very large profits, it was certainly important. The Associated Publishers, Inc.'s books were especially vital within the context of children's literature during the Harlem Renaissance. "Associated Publishers children's books responded to a powerful need within the young black community for books that would repair the psychological damage done by traditional textbooks," Katharine Capshaw Smith has argued. "In much of the children's literature extending from the New Negro Renaissance, school becomes a crucial site for the development of a progressive black identity, and nowhere is this phenomenon more pronounced than in the Associated Publishers material."[111] In 1950, Woodson's successor as director and editor, Rayford W. Logan, attested that "the Associated Publishers had a list of fourteen books written and edited by Dr. Woodson and more than fifty others by American, European and Latin American authors. The net impact of the *Journal* and these books upon historical scholarship in the United States and abroad is well-nigh incalculable."[112] In 1965, Benjamin Quarles added that the Associated Publishers, Inc., "lays claim to being the oldest publishing company of its kind...It has brought out more than 50 books, covering every major phase of Negro life and history."[113]

During Woodson's lifetime, 1538 Ninth Street, Northwest, functioned as an important mentoring center, "a training school for future historians" who learned "much from this master craftsman."[114] Jessie H. Roy, former student of Woodson at D.C.'s M Street High School in 1910, recalled how Woodson often invited her and others "to the office [to] continue our study of a character even if it meant staying until late in the night."[115] Woodson also used his residence as a meeting place, an informal intellectual movement center and a small warehouse for thousands of books, documents and archives pertaining to the history and culture of African descendants. By the mid-1920s, many donated important historical papers to the association to "preserve in its archives."

Between 1926 and 1950, it was Woodson's custom to convene meetings in the association's headquarters in order to organize Negro History Week celebrations and programs in Washington, D.C. In 1930, Lorenzo J. Greene recorded in his diary that he, Woodson, and others were busy working and planning in the office well past 1:00 a.m. upon many occasions. In 1925, days before the ASNLH had its tenth-anniversary annual meeting in Washington, D.C., dubbed "one of the most important ever held in the history of the race," the association featured an exhibition at the house. According to a 1925 *Washington Post* editorial, in Woodson's "office home" the ASNLH "presented an exhibition of 'engravings of the antique work of Benin, together with rare books and manuscripts.'"[116] While not a museum in the traditional sense, Woodson's home did function as an informal community-based museum, "a keeper of the culture" that grew "directly from the culture and history of African Americans" and a vital repository of historical materials and artifacts that Woodson collected and that were donated to the ASNLH. As more than a few of his co-workers observed and as several existing photos of Woodson in his home at his desk positioned in front of bookshelves reveal, all available space in the home was used to store manuscripts and documents.

Woodson's office-home clearly served many purposes. Nonetheless, by the early 1930s, Woodson dreamed of having more space. He proposed establishing an Institute of Negro Culture in Washington, D.C., to "foster the development of black music, drama, and art," envisioning "an auditorium for cultural programs, an exhibition area for artworks, and a library for rare books and manuscripts."[117] Though between 1929 and 1938 Woodson established a collection at the Library of Congress, he probably sought to have more control over this documentary trove and wanted the black community, especially in Washington, D.C., to have more access to these materials. According to Jacqueline Goggin, Woodson's 1934 request for funding from the Rockefeller's General Education Board ($2 million to start with) was very ambitious, and he did not seem angry when his proposal was unsurprisingly denied. Still, Woodson's proposal indicates how he imagined using space in Washington, D.C., to promote the cause of black history in a manner that was not possible in 1538 Ninth Street, Northwest. Woodson described his ideal Institute of Negro Culture:

> *A three-story stone and marble structure which embod[ies] the spirit of the undertaking and will lend tone to it, with an auditorium of a seating capacity of not less than three thousand, with adequate rooms for exhibits of all arts, with a library for rare books and manuscripts, and with lecturing halls for special instruction. The details to be worked out by the architect, who should be guided as much as possible by the outlines and purposes of the Belgium Congo Museum...[The]* cost to be two million dollars.[118]

Nevertheless, Woodson utilized the limited space that he had in many practical and creative ways. According to Mary Pearl Daugherty, who worked as a typist and secretary for Woodson from the fall of 1938 until the summer of 1941, Woodson wrote books in the comfort of his home. "He would walk around his office, his eyes closed and his hands clasped behind his back, crisply dictating. Sometimes he would dictate whole chapters of one of his books, without reference notes," an eighty-four-year-old Daugherty recalled in 2000. "Then, when I would show him the manuscript, he would say, 'Mrs. D., you split an infinitive!'" Other typists, secretaries and stenographers performed similar services in Woodson's home. Woodson ran the office with authority. One of Woodson's employees recalled, "We used to say at the office when Woodson spoke, no dog barked." Most of the young women who worked in his office were not well paid, usually in cash. Dorothy Revallion, who worked as a secretary and typist for Woodson for about five years during the 1920s,

Woodson in February 1948. *Scurlock Studio Records, ca. 1905–1994, Archives Center, National Museum of American History, Smithsonian Institution.*

threatened to quit because "she could not live upon her salary." The workdays in Woodson's office were often long. As Revallion experienced, "Woodson had also an irritating habit of dictating letters to his secretaries a little before closing time and insisting that they be gotten out before she left the office." One visitor to Woodson's office, taken aback by his abrasiveness, remarked: "Dr. Woodson should not meet visitors."[119]

There are very few existing descriptions of the actual physical conditions and layout of the association's headquarters during Woodson's lifetime, and Woodson did not elaborate on how he viewed his office-home. In passing in the *Norfolk Journal and Guide* in 1933, he described his role as being that of "caretaker" of 1538 Ninth Street, Northwest.[120] Contrary to the descriptions provided by his co-workers that depicted the third floor of the ASNLH's headquarters as being Woodson's personal apartment, he viewed it as being nothing more than an "attic" with which he made do. The third floor of Woodson's office-home had three rooms, one of which was used for storing books. Woodson slept in one of the other rooms and used the other as a living room of some sort. In 1953, L.D. Reddick recalled:

> *I found myself at 1538 Ninth Street, Northwest. This was the headquarters of the Association for the Study of Negro Life and History and the home of the* Journal of Negro History *and the other publications. The first floor was given over to the mail-order work of*

Lawrence Dunbar Reddick worked with Woodson and was greatly inspired by him. *Courtesy of Department of Special Collections, W.E.B Du Bois Library, University of Massachusetts Amherst.*

the Association. Woodson's office was on the second floor—and what an office! Books and magazines were piled everywhere (almost as bad as mine these days). Papers and letters and galley proofs covered the desk. But there seemed to be actually no disorder. The editor probably did more high grade work at that desk than any editor I know. Woodson lived, that is, slept, on the third floor of the small building.[121]

Two decades later, W. Montague Cobb, a former student of Woodson and one of the six pallbearers for Woodson's funeral, noted: "The quarters of the ASNLH at 1538 Ninth St., clearly showed the difference between form and substance. There was no money to spend on renovations so none were made. No one would scoff at the unpainted front or bare wooden floors, because the volumes and quality of work done in the house made any external trappings insignificant."[122] The basement of Woodson's office-home was used for storing books published by the Associated Publishers, Inc., and was not in the best shape. By the summer of 1930, books were literally rotting there. Fortunately, Lorenzo J. Greene was able to convince his elder to let him and four Howard University students conduct a cross-country book-selling campaign for the association from 1930 until 1933. The first floor included four rooms, a reception area, clerical space, a room for book orders and shipping and a small storage space. The second floor included Woodson's office, a kitchen, a library and more storage space for books.

Though he had many secretaries, assistants and co-workers, Woodson personally tended to the upkeep of the office. When he was out of town, his close research assistants were in charge of maintaining the office. Lorenzo J. Greene recalled:

Woodson was no snob, no work was too menial for him. Since Woodson could not afford to hire a janitor, not infrequently of a morning I encountered him attired in pajamas and a shabby bathrobe, broom and dustpan, or mop and pail in hand, cleaning the office. The climax came one morning when I found him down on his hands and knees oiling the floors, and of all things the floor of my office which adjoined his. Ashamed and embarrassed at seeing him do such lowly work, I volunteered to help. But he cut me short with: "Mr. Greene, I did not hire you to be a janitor."[123]

Greene added that Woodson often spoke with his employees in "his sanctum, the Kitchen" and used housework as relief from academic

This is a famous photo of Woodson in February 1948. *Scurlock Studio Records, ca. 1905–1994, Archives Center, National Museum of American History, Smithsonian Institution.*

work. Woodson outworked his protégé twenty-five years his junior. In his diary on September 11, 1928, Greene wrote, "We talked as Woodson painted. I admire him. No sort of work is too menial for him to perform. He likes to paint; it's a hobby of his. Says it is like a vacation."[124]

In 1991, four decades after Woodson's death, in the *Journal of Negro History*, Willie Leanna Miles, who worked with Woodson from 1943 until 1950, provided very revealing descriptions, including a detailed floor plan, of Woodson's "office home" as she called it. Miles recalled:

> *Dr. Woodson lived in the building where he worked. His bedroom and living room were on the third floor. The kitchen and bath were located on the second floor back. His office and library were on the second floor front. The first floor front and back was where order and shipping, processing of* The Negro History Bulletin *and* The Journal of Negro History *and other miscellaneous clerical work was accomplished. The basement and every other available space in the building were used for storage of books, Bulletins, Journals, etc.... My work space assignment was in Dr. Woodson's Library, 2ⁿᵈ floor front, opposite the staircase leading to the third floor. This allowed me an opportunity to hear conversations from his office. He seldom missed telling a visitor about the fact that he was once a coal miner and once earned a living as a garbage collector...The Associated Publishers and the Association for the Study of Negro Life and History occupied the same building.*[125]

THE WOODSON HOME SINCE 1950

According to the will that Woodson created on November 30, 1934, the possession of the property for his office-home was transferred to the ASNLH. The history of 1538 Ninth Street, Northwest, following Woodson's death is difficult to chart. But it is clear that Woodson's home gradually ceased to physically and symbolically embody the heart of the early black history movement.

Due to the sudden nature of Woodson's death, the association's executive council was unprepared. The members were understandably more concerned with maintaining the association than they were with the fate of Woodson's office-home. They certainly recognized the value of

annual convention in New York, active members of the association, especially members of the executive council, supported "the renovation and restoration of the Carter G. Woodson Home at 1538 9th, NW, Washington, D.C." It was also proposed "to have a monument erected to Woodson on a grassy plot located not far away from the Carter G. Woodson House which he occupied for so many years and which is

This photo shows the detail of the main façade entranceway at the Carter G. Woodson House at 1538 Ninth Street, Northwest, Washington, D.C. *Courtesy of the Library of Congress.*

Opposite: A photo of the Woodson home when it was no longer being used. *Courtesy of the Library of Congress.*

not a National Historic Landmark."[130] By the middle of 1980, ASALH received funding for the project of restoring the Woodson Home, and in the summer, "the U.S. Department of Interior, in cooperation with the District of Columbia Department of Housing and Human Resources, provided a grant of $38,000, later increased to $63,000."[131] About $8,000 was raised by ASALH fundraising efforts.

The Woodson Home was in sound enough shape to host the executive council for a tour and luncheon on June 14, 1980. After the meeting at the Carter G. Woodson Center, the executive council went to the Woodson Home that was "well on its way to being completely renovated and restored" and was "approximately 91% completed" by Bryant and Bryant, a Washington, D.C.–based black-owned construction company. According to the minutes of the June 14, 1980 executive council meeting:

> *The members of the Executive Council were given a tour of the facility from the third floor top to the basement. Many of the members became nostalgic as they walked through the building, recalling great moments with founder Carter G. Woodson who made his home and the Association office at 1538. After a period of much talk about the past and Dr. Woodson, luncheon was served. The food consisted of chicken and fish boxes, adorned with a salad and sodas. The scene was so rustic and so full of pathos that Dr. Bettye Gardner, of D.C., was moved to comment on the "picture presented by the Executive Council members sitting on sawhorses and amid piles of lumber."*

A Renovation and Restoration Committee concluded that, when renovated, the Woodson Home should be divided into three major rooms for *the Journal of Negro History*, the association offices and "the Community Project and Lectures." It supported restoring "as many rooms as possible," especially Woodson's library, and it was suggested that the first floor be named in honor of Willie Leanna Miles, who, at the time, had committed thirty-six years of service to the association. The Carter G. Woodson House Use Committee was also formed at this executive council meeting, and it was charged with providing more recommendations as to how to best use the Woodson Home.

At the sixty-fifth-annual ASNLH meeting in New Orleans, Louisiana, in 1980, the executive council had on its agenda, among other issues, "Restoration of the Carter G. Woodson Home." In 1981, the association announced that 1538 Ninth Street, Northwest, had been restored and "shines brightly in all of its pristine glory." There are few existing photos of the interior of the Woodson Home until January 2008, when Beyer Blinder Belle, Architects and Planners, LLP, completed the *Historic Structure Report of the Carter G. Woodson Home*. A 1981 *Negro History Bulletin* article, "National Shrine Carter G. Woodson House Restored to Original Beauty and Utility," featured rare photos of the interior of the home, including a photo of "the stair-case where Carter G. Woodson walked from his offices on the first and second floors to his bedroom on the third floor" and six pictures of different rooms in the Woodson Home that had been repaired, including Woodson's bedroom and private study, both located on the third floor. There was also a photo of a carpenter installing a sink on the second floor.

During the early 1980s, significant structural changes were made to the Woodson Home, including minor repairs such as painting, floor repairs and alterations with the plumbing. By 1983, the renovation of the Carter G. Woodson Home was "completed" and housed the national offices of the Afro-American Museum Association. Several years later, in inviting ASALH members to enjoy their stay in Washington, D.C., for the sixty-ninth-annual convention from October 17–21, 1984, an ASNLH branch president from Washington, D.C., ensured conference goers that they would enjoy visiting the Carter G. Woodson Home. There does not appear to be any provocative discussions of the Carter G. Woodson Home in the *Journal of Negro History* or the *Negro History Bulletin* during the second half of the 1980s or the 1990s. Yet it is clear that during the latter half of the 1980s, the association "rented the house to the publishers of *American Visions* magazine" and more interior alterations were done. In 1988, the National Park Service completed a field assessment that provided some detail about the conditions of the Woodson Home and a year later "the Association received a permit to do electrical work at the house which included the installation of fire alarm pull stations, control panel, and bells, the addition of new surface mounted outlets, and adding light fixtures."[132]

THE CARTER G. WOODSON HOME, NATIONAL HISTORIC SITE

Very little has been recorded about the usage and status of the Carter G. Woodson Home during the 1990s. During this decade we do know that a diverse group of people began to more openly voice concerns about the fate of this National Historic Landmark. In 1991, the Afro-American Institute for Historic Preservation and Community Development and the Institute for Urban Development Research at George Washington University produced the "Carter G. Woodson National Historic Site and Management Study." Washington, D.C. native and former civil rights activist Congresswoman Eleanor Holmes Norton was an important figure in the political movement to preserve the Carter G. Woodson Home during the 1990s. Five years after mayor of West Virginia Robert Nelson erected a life-size statue of Woodson on Hal Greer Boulevard in Huntington, West Virginia, on November 2, 1999, Norton introduced "The Carter G. Woodson Home National Historic Site Study Act of 1999" in the House of Representatives, calling on the Department of Interior to "study the feasibility and suitability of designating" the Woodson Home as "a national historic site within the National Park Service...so that the resources of the National Park Service will be available to preserve and maintain this national treasure."[133]

Fittingly, during Black History Month on February 15, 2000, H.R. 3201 was approved and passed, 413–1, resulting in the "Carter G. Woodson Home National Historic Site Study Act of 2000." The Committee on Energy and National Resources authorized the secretary of the interior "to prepare a resource study of the home of Dr. Carter G. Woodson to determine the suitability and feasibility of designating it as a unit of the National Park Service."[134] At the dawning of the new millennium, the National Park Service conducted a study of the house and its suitability for federal management, and a diverse group of Washington, D.C. community activists began to publicize the need to rescue Woodson's home. At the same time, the Woodson Home also received some negative publicity. Early in 2001, for instance, journalist Courtland Milloy penned a scathing and pessimistic essay in the *Washington Post* that chastised African Americans for the dilapidated state of the Carter G. Woodson Home. "But there is something about the condition of the home of the man who started it all—with its leaky roof and broken stained-glass panes—that suggests that, for all our prideful reflections, we have not learned much," Milloy proclaimed. "To see a klatch of young black men huddled in back of the Woodson house, smoking dope, is to be reminded of his classic work, 'The Mis-Education of the Negro.'...It would take about $5 million to turn this house into a state-of-the-art museum and research center. For African Americans, who have a combined annual income of more than $500 billion, that would be less than we spend on malt liquor in a week…This inability to get behind a deserving cause, fueled by the belief that nothing black is worth saving—our children least of all—has become a hallmark of today's 'miseducated Negro.'" Others echoed Milloy's sentiments.[135]

Responding to a national letter-writing campaign and the efforts of the National Park Service, the National Trust for Historic Preservation identified the Carter G. Woodson Home—which had been unoccupied for about a decade—as being one of the United States' eleven most endangered historic places in June 2001. In a 2002 *OAH Newsletter*, ASALH executive council member Felix L. Armfield acknowledged the Organization of American Historians' executive board's commitment to "the effort to help save this national treasure" and called on others to join the ASALH in the cause of restoring the home to "its original splendor" and creating "a Visitor Center and interpretive exhibits." Supporting this cause, in 2002, ASALH received grant money from the National Trust for Historic Preservation to make some basic repairs to the home. In 2001 and 2002, the National Park Service conducted a special resource study on the Woodson Home and determined that the Woodson Home was "nationally significant" and indeed suitable for designation as a unit of the National Park System. Several months after Norton called for the establishment of the Carter G. Woodson Home National Historic Site in the District of Columbia, on May 14, 2003 H.R. 1012 passed in the House and allowed the National Park System to acquire Woodson's Home as a National Historic Site unit.

In the summer of 2003, the ASALH executive council continued its efforts to memorialize the Woodson Home by "reaching out to the public for support in our ongoing campaign to make the home of Carter G. Woodson a national historic site."[136] In a detailed 2003 report accompanying H.R. 1012 (known as the Carter G. Woodson Home National Historic Site Establishment Act of 2003, filed at the end of July and printed a month later), the Committee on Energy and Natural Resources unanimously recommended that the H.R. 1012 be passed by the Senate. The Congressional Budget Office estimated that "implementing H.R. 1012 would cost the Federal Government $9.5 million over the next five years." Included in this budget was the acquisition of the Woodson Home and adjacent buildings; the restoration of the home and the development of interpretive exhibits; and the management, operation, researching and documenting of the site. In this report, the committee detailed the specifics of the act. The committee, for instance, indicated that the secretary of the interior "may acquire any of the 3 properties immediately north of the Carter G. Woodson Home located at 1540, 1542, and 1544 Ninth Street, Northwest"; that the Woodson Home would be administered like other units in the National Park System; that the secretary of the interior was required to prepare a general management plan within three years after receiving the funding to do so; and that the ASALH would have the opportunity to perhaps use parts of the Woodson Home for its administrative purposes and would play an advisory role in the administration of the site.[137]

Months later, on December 19, 2003, the Carter G. Woodson Home was formally designated a National Historic Site, and on February 27, 2006, the building was "officially" dedicated as the Carter G. Woodson Home National Historic Site, a distinct unit of the National Park Service, the 389th unit of the National Park System. On June 10, 2005, the National Park Service purchased the Woodson Home from ASALH for $465,000, and on January 15, 2008, Beyer Blinder Belle, Architects and Planners, LLP, produced an exhaustive *Historic Structure Report for the Carter G. Woodson Home*. During the last several years, the ASALH, the Organization of American Historians and the National Park Service have played key roles in the movement to restore and memorialize the Woodson Home. As a writer in a 2008 volume of *National Parks: The Magazine of the National Parks Conservation Association* asserted: "When the Park Service unveils the Carter G. Woodson Home as a National Historic Site in Washington D.C.'s Shaw neighborhood (with luck, sometime before 2015), the residence of one of American history's unsung heroes, Dr. Carter G. Woodson, will finally be made public. And with that, there is hope that Woodson's lifework will at last be given the recognition it deserves."[138] At the same time, in December 2012, Congresswomen Eleanor Holmes Norton grew impatient with the National Park Service and sent a letter to President Barack Obama, requesting that he "see to it that the appropriate officials develop a strategy and timeline for completing the Carter G. Woodson project" with "the high priority it deserves."

3

"BECAUSE OF HIS SELFLESS DEDICATION TO THE WORK OF THE ASSOCIATION"

Woodson's "Mass Education Movement"

Real history requires the elimination of self. Facts must be set forth with objectivity. History must be kept out of the atmosphere of agitation and propaganda. It is not a question as to what the teacher or leader of a group may think about things but what the person taught will think about them when he has learned the facts for himself. Every person under instruction must be given credit for having sense enough to make an inference. Facts set properly forth will tell their own story.
—Carter G. Woodson, 1938

We must go back to the achievements of these black men, then, and looking into these black faces of heroes and heroines, get inspiration to achieve as well as they did. With a vision of these great souls looking down upon us and urging us on to complete the unfinished task to the performance of which they made an outstanding contribution, let us press forward to the next objective in the development and uplift of the despised and rejected of men.
—Carter G. Woodson, 1932

Taken together, the two citations above from the 1930s epitomize Woodson's philosophy of the purpose of history. Foremost, he viewed black history as a scholarly enterprise. He also enlisted history as a practical tool for black psychological uplift and empowerment. After founding the ASNLH and increasingly by the 1920s, Woodson blended and balanced these two ideologies. He consistently believed that history was a necessary ingredient to African Americans' self-knowledge and collective identity. One of his most famous sayings was "If a race has no history, if it has not worth-while tradition, it becomes a negligible factor in the thought of the world, and it stands in the danger of being exterminated."[139] Woodson perceived black history as being an essential part of American history. In a 1927 Negro History Week circular, he underscored: "We should emphasize not Negro History, but the Negro in history. What we need is not a history of selected races or nations, but the history of the world void of national bias, race hate, and religious prejudice. There should be no indulgence in undue eulogy of the Negro. The case of the Negro is well taken care of when it is shown how he has influenced the development of civilization."[140]

Woodson routinely underscored that the purpose of black history was not to focus on how blacks had been victimized but instead on how blacks had influenced U.S. and world history. Woodson insisted, "The aim has been to emphasize important facts in the belief that facts properly set forth will speak for themselves."[141] As he announced during Negro History Week celebrations, Woodson was opposed to opportunists within the black community who used fictional or hyperbolized expressions of black history as a form of propaganda or black cultural nationalism. In the *Norfolk Journal and Guide* in 1936, Woodson warned:

> *Because the public is gullible it will seize upon almost any thing labeled as history. Negroes, themselves, then are doing much to discredit the effort to set forth in scientific form what the race has thought and felt and attempted and accomplished. Certain Negro writers are using the opportunity as a racket to sell the public the spectacular for whatever cash may be obtained therefrom. Often the Association is called upon to evaluate these unscientific efforts, but most of them are not worthy of a criticism.*[142]

One of Woodson's most important contributions to the early black history movement was his mission and ability to employ black history as a medium for uplifting blacks and challenging racial prejudice. Especially after founding Negro History Week, he successfully transformed his early black history movement into a mass movement of some sort. After Woodson severed ties from white philanthropists, the association was forced to rely upon black communities throughout the nation for support, and he, in turn, actively solicited their support and praised their efforts. In 1947, Woodson recounted:

Believing that the Negroes as a mass should do something material for the advancement of this work, numerous schools and colleges have staged local drives and penny collections to aid the work which the Association has been promoting these thirty-two years in spite of many handicaps. A teacher in a rural school takes up a penny collection among her forty pupils and adds twenty-five cents or a dollar and sends it to the national office in Washington. The amount contributed is small, but the lesson in self-help may be far-reaching. Years hence the pupils who gave only a penny each may give thousands to a worthy cause.[143]

Woodson strove to enlighten the black masses, popularizing black history in a variety of innovative ways. In addition to rooting the ASNLH in black community infrastructures, he initiated Negro History Week and other extension services and founded the *Negro History Bulletin*. Equally important, as he articulated in no uncertain terms in *The Mis-Education of the Negro*, Woodson dictated that his PhD-holding contemporaries apply their specialized academic training to the black struggle and commit themselves to working with and in behalf of the black masses.

Woodson produced accessible historical scholarship that was aimed at attracting a wide readership from elementary school students to university students, such as *The Negro in Our History* (1922), *Negro Makers of History* (1928), *African Myths Together with Proverbs* (1928), *The African Background Outlined* (1936) and *African Heroes and Heroines* (1939). The unfinished *Encyclopedia Africana* was also written in a very simple language. Woodson valued his basic African American history textbooks. Several years before it was actually published, Woodson advertised *The Negro in Our History* as a study for use in black history clubs, elementary and high schools and colleges and universities. "Just as soon as this book has come from the press," Woodson announced, "the Association will send to all Negro schools of secondary and college grade a field agent to interest them in the effort to inculcate in the mind of the youth of African blood an appreciation of what their race has thought and felt and done."[144]

It is difficult to discern how black youth and laypersons were impacted by Woodson's writings. The exhaustive *Papers of Carter G. Woodson and the Association for the Study of Negro Life and History, 1915–1950* contains elaborate records of books sold by the association. While there are countless receipts and order forms, the Associated Publishers struggled to sell books. Working-class blacks, especially during the lean years of the Great Depression, did not place a high priority on purchasing scholarly literature. It appears that black professionals usually purchased the association's literature. By March of 1941, 40,000 copies of *The Negro in Our History* had been sold. By 1950, one journalist noted that *Negro Makers of History* had sold nearly 100,000 copies.

Woodson's most famous and effective black history popularization effort was through Negro History Week celebrations. But before 1926, when he inaugurated this celebration, Woodson spoke at countless venues throughout his lifetime for minimal fees. He also corresponded with innumerable men and women from all around the world interested in black history. Early on in the association's history, Woodson sought to gain a mass following with outreach programs and the promotion of black history clubs. Several years before the first Negro History Week celebration, he commented that he had succeeded in convincing schools and colleges to "devote more time to the study of Negro life and history" and that "a larger number of persons" were becoming interested in the association's work. By the mid-1920s, Woodson remarked that ASNLH black history clubs existed in practically all U.S. cities with considerable black populations.

Woodson founded Negro History Week in 1926. He explained the reason behind the celebration in a pamphlet "widely distributed" months before the first celebration was to take place during the second week in February 1926, in commemoration of Frederick Douglass's and Abraham Lincoln's birthdays. He exclaimed that blacks knew "practically nothing" about their history. He ultimately believed that African Americans could benefit immensely from knowledge of their past and the accomplishments of their ancestors.[145] He added that race prejudice was the byproduct of whites' beliefs that black people had not contributed anything of worth to world civilization. He argued that if the historical record was set straight and that if the history of black people were studied along with the achievements of others in schools, not only would black youth develop a sense of pride and self-worth, but racism would also be abolished. Woodson concluded: "Let truth destroy the dividing prejudice of nationality and teach universal love without distinction of race, merit or rank. With sublime enthusiasm and heavenly vision of the Great Teacher let us help men rise above the race hate of their age unto the altruism of a rejuvenated universe."[146]

Negro History Week was the first major achievement in popularizing black history and was unique in that it focused on the black youth. Woodson realized that the mis-education of black people began in

This engraved portrait of Frederick Douglass appeared in his *My Bondage and My Freedom* published in 1855. Woodson selected the second week in February for Negro History Week in honor of Douglass's birth. *Courtesy of Wikimedia Commons.*

their homes, communities and elementary schools. Woodson's vision of Negro History Week was optimistic, strategic and long term. He wanted this modest, weeklong celebration to serve as a steppingstone toward the gradual introduction of black history into the curricula of all levels of the U.S. educational system. He hoped that Negro History Week would evolve into "Negro History Year," as he affirmed from time to time. Woodson consistently instructed those observing the week that they needed to diligently prepare for the celebration months in advance and that after mid-February, they needed to continue acknowledging the role of African descendants in world history. "Negro History Week should be a demonstration of what has been done in the study of the Negro during the year and at the same time as a demonstration of greater things to be accomplished," Woodson instructed school teachers. "A subject which receives attention one week out of the thirty-six will not mean much to anyone."[147]

According to Woodson, soon after he mailed out his first "Negro History Week Circulars" to various educational institutions, presses, fraternal and social welfare organizations, literary societies and radio stations, "there was a stir in the direction of active participation." He boasted, "There were few places in the country where this celebration did not make some impression."[148] Woodson offered those who decided to participate in Negro History Week celebrations promotional materials and resources. He also gave many suggestions.

In pamphlets and articles in the *Negro History Bulletin*, as well as in editorials in numerous black newspapers, he routinely instructed participants to organize committees for the celebration months before Negro History Week. He outlined the critical steps to success: involving the governing, power-wielding board of education; advertising the events extensively; recording oral testimonies from elders within the community; persuading libraries to order black history books; setting aside one day of every week as a "Book and Picture Fund Day" to raise money to purchase black history books for the community; sending any relevant historical documents to the association so that they could be properly maintained; organizing black history clubs; and creating a pageant highlighting the struggles of black Americans. He always offered special suggestions to schoolteachers about maximizing the involvement of the youth in practical ways, especially in February volumes of the *Bulletin*.

During the celebrations there were banquets, breakfasts, speeches, parades, exhibits and lectures that were usually held in churches, black colleges and universities and community centers. Woodson insisted that a significant number of the events be free to the public. For this week, he stressed that speakers and organizers should donate their time to the cause. Schoolteachers, mainly black women, were vital Negro History Week organizers. They raised funds in their communities and got their students involved in the week's activities.

After its inception in 1926, Negro History Week continued to expand. In his annual reports of the director, Woodson routinely noted that every year, Negro History Week drew a greater following. In many volumes of the *Journal of Negro History*, Woodson devoted brief articles to describing the success of the various programs. He was very pleased that Negro History Week had eventually made its way into the black churches, self-help organizations, public schools and even to rural areas. In 1932, he also noted that Negro History Week was finding its way into white schools, facilitating better "inter-racial relations." With each passing year, the black and occasionally the white press advertised local and national events. The most active presses in helping publicize Woodson's movement early on included the *Philadelphia Tribune*, the *Baltimore Commonwealth*, the *Chicago Defender*, the *Palmetto Leader*, the *Tampa Bulletin*, the *Washington Eagle* and the *Norfolk Journal and Guide*. Other widely distributed newspapers later joined in advertising Negro History Week. Various radio stations were instrumental in publicizing and broadcasting Negro History Week events.

By the 1940s, Negro History Week celebrations were increasingly popular. Woodson developed elaborate programming schedules. In November 1948, in order to help rural schools with little or no resources, he introduced Negro History Week Kits at $2.00 apiece. At first, the kits included writings and speeches by famous blacks as well as a play depicting black history. Two years later, they were revised by Woodson to also include many photos of famous blacks as well as a list of books for further research. The cost for this edition was $2.50. For Woodson, it was essential for the people themselves, especially the children, to create their own unique, personalized celebrations. In October 1941, he offered the following advice to schoolteachers: "Do not call in some silver-tongued orator to talk to your school about the history of the Negro. The orator does not generally have much in his head. His chief qualification is strong lungs—a good bellows. He knows very little about things in general and practically nothing about the Negro in particular except how to exploit the race. Let the children study the history of the race, and they will be the speakers who will put the spellbinder to shame."[149]

As Negro History Week became more popular, Woodson believed that there was a class of people who were exploiting the celebration for their own benefit. Woodson routinely warned the public about "the disastrous methods of pseudo-historians among Negroes exaggerating in spectacular fashion facts of minor importance" in order to capitalize on a movement and transform it into a commercial venture. He was especially enraged with those "impostors" and "mis-informants," mainly entertainers, who, under the name of the ASNLH, made large profits from Negro History Week events. At one point, he even demanded that they turn over their earnings to the association, and he called on Negro History Week organizers to boycott those "mischievous orators" and instead call on one of the many historians whom Woodson trained.[150]

Negro History Week was a monumental educational and cultural movement. Assessing the impact of Negro History Week celebrations on black working-class and youth consciousness from 1926 until 1950 is challenging. Nonetheless, we can assume that many of those blacks who took part in these events felt great pride in their heritage and that some open-minded whites who witnessed and helped sponsor such events may have changed their views of black history and culture.

Schoolchildren were probably the most highly transformed by these events. They learned by doing, researching the lives of famous blacks and acting in plays that depicted the African-American past. Throughout the late 1930s and 1940s, many female schoolteachers wrote to Woodson sharing with him, often in great detail, how they conducted their Negro History Week celebrations and how the processes had influenced them and others. Woodson often published these commentaries in the *Bulletin*. Many testified that Negro History Week had helped transform their cultural and political consciousness.

Many of Woodson's colleagues also believed that Negro History Week was his "most characteristic creation." Devoted Negro History Week promoter Luther Porter Jackson called Negro History Week "the feeder for every other activity of the Association." In paying tribute to the association founder, L.D. Reddick noted that "his greatest influence upon the public mind came through Negro History Week." Reddick believed that the effect of Negro History Week on African Americans' self-confidence, poise, desire to achieve and morale "defies measurement." This "mass education program" and "God-send for the Association" pleased Woodson to "no end," and on several occasions, he deemed it the association's most valuable contribution. Woodson extended himself during this month. In 1933, during the peak of the Great Depression, he spent not only the week of Negro History Week lecturing at various venues but also the next month "in the field," lecturing and helping people organize throughout the country. "By far," Woodson noted in the early 1930s, "the greatest stimulus given to the educational work of the Association in recent years has been the observance of Negro History Week."[151]

In 1927, a year after the founding of Negro History Week, Woodson established the association's Extension Division in order to expose more people to black history through public lectures and correspondence study. The Home Study Department was necessary in Woodson's view because it could educate teachers who would then in turn teach the black youth about their history and because "various classes of citizens" needed to know their history. This process of education involves the passing on of information through a series of closely interactive stages and levels. The Home Study Program took the school to the student. Woodson's program offered courses at introductory and advanced levels. Only those with a high school education and the desire to "profit by the work" were encouraged to apply for admission. One had to apply for admission and pay a five-dollar matriculation fee. Tuition for one course was twenty dollars. Two classes could be taken for thirty-five dollars, and three classes could be taken for fifty-two dollars. Students had a maximum of one year to finish the requirements for each course, including the passing of a final examination. Woodson encouraged students to complete the assigned work in two to three months.[152] In October 1927, under the heading "To Offer Extension Courses in Negro Life and History," the *Pittsburgh Courier* advertised this program.

Each introductory course was accompanied by a series of lessons with specific readings and suggestions. After completing these lessons, the student would, ideally, answer some questions and mail the "recitation paper" back to the instructor, who would then review it and mail it back to the student with the appropriate comments. Advanced courses were offered to college graduates. Woodson arranged the classes with input from both the students and the professors and assured the public that the standards of the Home Study Department were equal to those of "accredited colleges and universities," that "nothing is hastily done" and that "every student is guaranteed personal attention." A brochure for the Home Study Department offered anthropology, art, English, history, literature and sociology. The teaching staff included leading scholars, such as Woodson himself, Charles H. Wesley, Alain Locke, E. Franklin Frazier, Luther Porter Jackson, James Hugo Johnston and Charles Johnson. At the end of the course, each student received a certificate noting the amount of work that was completed. Full credit was granted only to those who passed the final examination. The Home Study Department did not appear to be successful in terms of enrollment. While Woodson noted that the second year of the Home Study Department went "remarkably well," a year later, he admitted that the enrollment was very low mainly because of the fees and the standards of admission.

By the mid 1930s, Woodson wanted to increase his regular readership among black youth, the black working-class, black elementary and secondary schoolteachers and non-academics in general. The *Journal of Negro History* was inaccessible to many because of its intellectual content, and it was relatively expensive. The *Bulletin* was the vehicle by which schoolteachers and other concerned citizens could take black history into the homes of the black masses. The magazine served as an advertising mechanism for the ASNLH's activities, especially for Negro History Week. It also served as a forum with which African American elementary schoolchildren, community activists, schoolteachers and professional scholars could openly discuss and make known their thoughts about black history. Woodson also wrote opinion columns in the *Bulletin*.

The first issue of the *Bulletin* was released in October 1937 and, like the rest of the volumes during Woodson's lifetime, appeared nine times throughout the year, coinciding with the months of the school year. Until the late 1940s, a year's subscription was one dollar (or twelve to fifteen cents a copy). Woodson also offered bulk rate discounts, and for some time, clubs of five people or more could secure the magazine for only forty-five cents a year. By 1950, the subscription price had risen only to two dollars a year, or twenty-five cents a copy. Woodson kept the price low (and in fact sold the magazine at a loss) in order to maintain a higher readership. Though he was the managing editor, the editorial and managing boards were dominated by black women. They wrote many of the articles, organized and ran the magazine and encouraged children to begin their historical studies early. Individual issues of the *Bulletin* focused on certain topics and themes in black American history. Woodson did this so that regular subscribers would have "a brief illustrated history of the Negro" at the end of the year. He also sold back issues bound in one volume.

Between 1937 and 1950, issues contained biographical sketches of famous and not so famous blacks and whites who were sentimental to the cause; short book reviews; questions for the readers; numerous photographs; discussions of periods and important events in black history; updates about current events mainly pertaining to black schools, Negro History Week, branches and clubs; artwork by leading black artists; a "Book of the Month" section; poetry; information about African peoples; suggestions for Negro History Week; short black history plays; and primary sources.

Woodson at his desk in 1948 with copies of the *Negro History Bulletin. Scurlock Studio Records, ca. 1905–1994, Archives Center, National Museum of American History, Smithsonian Institution.*

The *Bulletin* aimed at instilling "the youth of African blood" with pride in their history and culture. In October 1941, a formal "Children's Page" was introduced. The female editorial staff as well as other female readers suggested to Woodson that a section of the magazine be officially designated for children. In November 1940, for instance, Lillian M. Rhoades, the associate editor of *Apex News*, told Woodson that she would like for the *Bulletin* "to solicit verse and articles by children." She reasoned: "This column devoted to their contributions will get them interested in

Artist Lois Mailou Jones (shown here in 1936 or 1937) played an important role with the *Negro History Bulletin. Courtesy of the National Archives and Records Administration.*

their particular page, and familiar with the *Journal* as a whole. Then as they grow up," she continued, "they will grow up with the *Journal*, and would not be without it."[153] The thoughts, prose and ideas of children were often featured in the *Bulletin* as a method of influencing other youngsters to seriously study black history. Each issue's "Children's Section" challenged readers to answer questions pertaining to the monthly theme and quizzed about how they could best facilitate a Negro History Week celebration. Under the guidance of Howard University artist Lois Mailou Jones, the young readers during the early 1940s were encouraged to study African American history through various creative art projects and exercises.

Teachers benefited immensely from the *Bulletin*. In its pages, they discussed how to best incorporate black history into their individual classrooms and their schools' curriculums, exchanged teaching methods and shared advice about how to best celebrate Negro History Week. In a sense, the pages of the *Bulletin* truly belonged to black schoolteachers, and Woodson took their contributions seriously. From time to time, he solicited and published their suggestions. The *Bulletin* was unique in that it was one of the only journals open to black female teachers. He included photographs of them in the midst of other movers and shakers in the struggle.

In every issue of the *Bulletin*, Woodson wrote at least one column. He constantly reminded bulletin readers that the purpose of Negro History Week was not to simply acknowledge and celebrate blacks' accomplishments for one week. Woodson's straightforward philosophy of history as explained in the *Bulletin* was very non-elitist. He believed that anyone willing to invest significant work could "act like" a historian. In 1943, the association founder told teachers that a historian was a rigorous collector and organizer of facts, that children could be historians by recording their families' pasts and that even those not formally educated could be historians of some sort by writing down, in whatever language, the histories of their communities. Woodson firmly held that the history of black Americans, despite their oral traditions, needed to be recorded by black people.

Woodson also used the *Bulletin* to criticize white America for mistreating blacks while celebrating blacks' abilities to persevere and to critique his fellow black Americans, especially black intellectuals, the black middle-class, black businessmen and the type of black preacher who, "after he receives his collection...is ready to retire to some other part of the city because he does not care to dwell in their district."[154] During the era of World War II, Woodson's commentaries took on a much more political flavor. He indicted the U.S. government for mistreating devoted black soldiers during and after the war. He declared in one column that U.S. policies "resembled more the policies of Hitler" than those of a so-called democratic nation. To Woodson, this behavior conformed with the historical abuse endured by black American soldiers since the colonial era. Like many other black leaders throughout history and his time, he publicized and supported blacks' historical and contemporary activities in the armed forces in hopes that blacks would receive citizenship in exchange for their services. Embracing the "Double V Campaign," he believed that the black soldier's loyalty during World War II would "strengthen his case" for equality and first-class citizenship.[155]

Throughout the remainder of the 1940s, Woodson continued to publish social commentaries in the *Bulletin*. He attacked segregation in American social and institutional life, condemned America's imperialist and expansionist ethos in the immediate aftermath of World War II, scrutinized problems plaguing the black community from within, reiterated and clarified the function of Negro History Week and commented on the changes affecting black people in a global context.

During Woodson's lifetime, the *Bulletin* underwent various changes and developments. The first major change, in October 1939, was the increase in size from eight to sixteen pages. Woodson resolved that black schoolteachers were in need of more information to adequately incorporate black history into their curriculums. Woodson did not increase the price, and by the magazine's third volume, the articles were becoming more in-depth, thematically organized and more scholarly in tone. During the 1940s, more than a few of Woodson's protégés wrote essays for the magazine. By October 1940, the style of the magazine changed. While the first three volumes resembled a small newspaper, the volumes after 1940 looked more like a journal or magazine, resembling issues of *The Crisis*.

Woodson believed that the *Bulletin* was a successful venture. In 1943, he declared that "nothing attempted" by the ASNLH since Negro History Week "has met with more public approval" than the *Bulletin*. He felt justified in publishing it at a loss because he believed that it was finding its ways into the minds of black people, making black schoolteachers more well rounded, inspiring black youth and even helping to deconstruct race prejudice and foster better relations between blacks and whites. The *Bulletin* was one of Woodson's most significant black history popularization efforts. John Hope Franklin certainly thought so. "The BULLETIN," Franklin noted, "represented perhaps the most vigorous extension of the work of Dr. Woodson into the lives of persons who were soon to share the responsibility of making their communities better places in which to live."[156]

4

CHIPPING PAST THE "FORBIDDING EXTERIOR"

The Father of Black History Remembered

In order to best understand the intricacies of Woodson's personality and commitment to black history, it is helpful to revisit the existing recollections of Woodson. While many of Woodson's contemporaries and protégés have written about their experiences with him, the importance of Lorenzo J. Greene's observations in his diary on June 27, 1928, cannot be underemphasized: "I told Miss Revallion she should have kept a diary during her four years here. After Woodson's death it would become invaluable to anyone who desired to write his life."[157] As Willie L. Miles observed, as a secretary, "you actually learned the interworkings of the Associated Publishers and the Association for the Study of Negro Life and History from taking dictation from Dr. Woodson."[158]

Woodson was remembered by different people in different ways. As Greene noted, "It is virtually impossible to evaluate a personality as intricate as that of Dr. Woodson." Few "really knew him."[159] Most tended to agree that he was a physically fit and stubborn "hard man" who enjoyed researching, traveling, talking and walking. "Few, if any, took the liberty to call him 'Carter.'"[160] Mary McLeod Bethune and Nannie Helen Burroughs were the only ones to call him by his first name. Most others addressed him as Dr. Woodson. While many have concurred that he was stern, serious, single-minded, cantankerous and impatient with those who were not as committed to his "life-and-death struggle" as he was, in 1958, *Ebony* perhaps stretched the truth a bit in proclaiming that he had "few friends," "never consciously sought to be liked" and "never

Left: Nannie Helen Burroughs, the founder of the National Training School for Women and Girls in Washington, D.C., required her students to study African American history before graduating. *Courtesy of the Library of Congress*.

Opposite: Mary McLeod Bethune served as president of the ASNLH from 1936 until 1952. This photograph was taken by Gordon Parks in 1943. *Courtesy of the Library of Congress*.

cultivated those habits and personality traits which would endear him to the public." ASNLH co-founder and close friend of Woodson James E. Stamps certainly disagreed with this portrayal. In 1965, he recalled: "It was my privilege then to know Woodson. Walking and talking were his favorite recreations...Most of us, a bit younger than Woodson, loved his wit, his humor and even his sarcasm. If you did not know him his sharp tongue could hurt you, but whatever he said was a gem." Woodson also had a soft spot in his heart for children.

Following his death, Woodson was remembered by his co-workers, friends and disciples. Most of the published recollections were celebrations of the deceased founder of the ASNLH, with the exception of critical appraisals by a few of his "Boys" and W.E.B. Du Bois. In the dawning of the 1950s, Rayford W. Logan, Mary McLeod Bethune and Charles H. Wesley published brief accounts of their deceased friend and mentor in the *Journal of Negro History*. Wesley's article was the most in-depth. In Wesley's estimation, Woodson was "a Discoverer of the Truth" who "did not want the Negro people to meet 'the awful fate of becoming a negligible factor in the thought of the world'" and who "never hesitated

to abandon the false for the true, whatever the cost to him or the cause"; "a Contributor to Truth" by publishing and editing extensively; "an Organizer of Truth" who left behind a movement; "a Disseminator of Truth" to scholarly and unscholarly audiences; and "a Fighter for Truth" who fought all "traducers" of the race, regardless of race or class.[161] Accounts in the *Negro History Bulletin* tended to praise Woodson. The May

1950 edition was dedicated to him, and Mary McLeod Bethune, John Hope Franklin, L.D. Reddick, Arnett G. Lindsay, Alrutheus A. Taylor and Langston Hughes shared their fond recollections of Woodson.

L.D. Reddick published one of the first articles in the *Negro History Bulletin* after 1950 that critically portrayed Woodson. "If anything, Woodson was forthright. Much of his stimulation to others came by way of challenge. He had little more than contempt for pretense or excuses," Reddick recalled. "Those who did not know him too well considered him to be a 'hard' man—and, upon occasion, he could be as cantankerous and as irascible as they came." Still, Reddick remembered how much he profited from "the good Doctor" in their long "engaging" discussions when Reddick visited the D.C. area from his former residence in New York. Reddick speculated that his mentor was naturally driven to such accomplishments by his childhood, adolescence and early adulthood experiences; his "rugged" health; and his commitment to a solid set of principles.[162]

Editorials in the *Negro History Bulletin* routinely saluted its founder, but between the magazine's May 1950 edition and historian Earl E. Thorpe's pioneering 1958 publication on black historians, only a handful of scholars commented on Woodson's contributions. One of these assessments was John Hope Franklin's 1957 "The New Negro History" published first in *The Crisis*. Franklin credited Woodson for "launching the era of 'The New Negro History.'" He posited that the new movement sprung from a combination of factors of American life, but he underscored Woodson's and the association's work. Franklin insisted:

> *This* [Woodson's efforts] *was, perhaps, the most far-reaching and ambitious effort to rewrite history that has ever been attempted in this country. But it was more than an attempt to rewrite history. It was a remarkable attempt to rehabilitate a whole people—to explode racial myths, to establish a secure and respectable place for the Negro in the evolution of the American social order, to develop self-respect and self-esteem among those who had been subjected to the greatest indignities known in the Western world. Finally, it was a valiant attempt to force America to keep faith with herself, to remind her that truth is more praiseworthy than power, and that justice and equality, long the state policy of this nation, should apply to all its citizens and even to the writing of history.*[163]

During the 1960s, there were no major studies published on Woodson. Yet in 1965, at the fiftieth-anniversary annual meeting of the association in Atlanta, there was a "Carter G. Woodson Memorial Session" with tributes presented by James E. Stamps, Willie Miles, William H. Brewer, Louis R. Mehlinger, Lorenzo J. Greene, C. Walker Thomas and Harry V. Richardson. Those who attended this session certainly benefited from these ASNLH members' recollections.

The 1965 special summer issue of the *Negro History Bulletin* celebrated fifty years of the association, and Charles H. Wesley (who had his fair share of serious conflicts with Woodson) sought to make sense of his elder's peculiar personality. He noted:

> *Despite the founding associates, Woodson, our Founder, belonged to the list of post–nineteenth century pioneer personalities in the techniques of American life who believed that it was necessary to work one's plan alone. He had, in this respect, a type of intolerance and self-opinion, which some of us regarded with humor and indulgence because we looked upon the cause as well as the man as equally valuable. This was an aspect of rugged individualism, which has helped to create the greatness of our nation through individual initiative and energy. He belonged to the era, the earmarks of which we hope have not entirely disappeared, when the individual will endeavor to be creative in his contributions and not to act so as merely to imitate the work launched by another.*[164]

Included in this volume are other valuable insights into Woodson's personality. Jessie H. Roy, for instance, recalled how Woodson actively mentored her and other black women.[165] In the twenty-eighth volume of the *Bulletin*, Lorenzo J. Greene shared some of his experiences with Woodson in 1930 from his detailed diary. In this particular entry, Greene "marveled" at Woodson's leadership and devotion to black history.[166] The remainder of Greene's journal was published in two volumes several decades later by historian Arvarh Strickland. Greene was much more critical of Woodson in a paper, "Dr. Carter G. Woodson: The Man As I Knew Him," that he delivered at various venues from the mid-1960s until the early 1980s.

Greene's unpublished essay is one of the most candid assessments of Woodson's character. Greene worked for Woodson and the ASNLH from 1928 until 1933 as a field investigator, a book salesman and an office employee. Though this document is undated and was presented and revised more than a few times by Greene during the 1960s, 1970s and 1980s, there is strong evidence that Greene first delivered this paper at the semicentennial celebration of the ASNLH in Atlanta, Georgia. Though never published, Greene's recollections are very important in unearthing and reconstructing Woodson's character in all its complexity.

Greene shared many positive memories about "the master," such as his endless devotion to "the cause"; his "forceful, sincere, clear, and convincing speaking abilities"; his unmatched work ethic; his isolated acts of extreme kindness; his "phenomenal memory"; his love of children; and his modesty. He also stressed:

> *Dr. Woodson was a complex, many-sided man...many admired Woodson, but few could love him. It was certainly so with me... Woodson had little consideration for the feelings of his co-workers. On several occasions when he cruelly hurt me, I remained faithful to him but only because of the movement that he personified. He was egotistic, opinionated, truculent, sarcastic, vindictive and at times seemed to take a sadistic delight in offending or hurting persons. We used to say at the office when Woodson spoke, no dog barked.*

Greene underscored his point, noting: "Woodson often disparaged and derided his associates. He seemed to take pleasure in crushing any vestige of self-confidence in them."[167] Greene shared many personal experiences and those of other employees to validate his claims. He added that as an employer, Woodson paid his employees little, pressured and overworked them and fired them suddenly, exemplified in his own case and that of Charles H. Wesley. Attempting to explain the origins of Woodson's peculiar personality, Greene surmised:

> *Despite the obvious greatness of the man and the adulation heaped upon him, deep down within, I believe Dr. Woodson was obsessed by a feeling of insecurity. It may have stemmed from the deprivation of his childhood. At any rate, his seeming compulsion to disparage, humiliate, even hurt those who worked closely with him led some of us to wonder whether he feared lest some younger man might push him from his intellectual stool and usurp his position.*[168]

After hearing Greene deliver this paper in 1983, a cousin of Woodson's told Greene, "That was Carter G. Woodson."

In 1971, Patricia Romero completed the first major scholarly biography on Woodson. For her dissertation, she interviewed many of Woodson's family members and co-workers. She briefly touched on Woodson's personality. "The birth of the *Journal* was to Woodson literally something more than a mere publishing event; throughout his life he devoted himself to the *Journal* as most men would to a family," Romero suggested. "When he had conflicts with other men, or organization[s], he would turn to the 'Notes' section of the *Journal* to unburden himself. A lonely man except for his work, he used the *Journal* as some men might a wife as an emotional outlet." Romero's point is well taken. A significant part of Woodson's personality can be reconstructed through an examination of the journal. Romero clearly admired Woodson, but her biography is by no means uncritical or celebratory. She cited the criticisms of men like Victor Daly, who asserted that Woodson "was a hard man to get along with. He was not a lover of his fellow man."[169]

In 1972, Woodson's immediate successor as association director, Rayford W. Logan, published a thoughtful paper first delivered before the fifty-seventh annual meeting of the ASNLH in Cincinnati, Ohio. "It is hoped," Rayford W. Logan humbly announced, "that this lecture will suggest the need for further investigation that will result in an authoritative biography."[170] Logan grappled with how Woodson's experiences before the founding of the association impacted his unwavering character established thereafter. In 1983, Sister Anthony Scally published the first full-length biography on Woodson, *Walking Proud: The Story of Dr. Carter G. Woodson*. She interviewed Woodson's relatives, combed through various archives and corrected some inconsistencies generated by previous scholarship. Scally's study was further authenticated by her experience working as a librarian for the ASNLH and as a regular contributor to the *Bulletin*.

In the mid-1980s, the association organized several panel discussions on its founder at various meetings. In December 1984, the association had a "Day of Commemoration for Woodson" at the association headquarters. The program for the event included six accounts of Woodson from those who knew him best, recognition of honorees and various exhibits featuring Woodson artifacts, memorabilia and books by and about him. Those who attended certainly heard more intimate stories about this man who kept largely to himself. About a year later, the association had a seminar on Woodson at its annual meeting that included as panelists L.D. Reddick, John Hope Franklin, Dorothy Porter Wesley, Arnett Lindsay and Lorenzo J. Greene. Nonetheless, in 1984, Greene lamented: "The real biography of Woodson remains to be written and, unfortunately, those who held the key to Woodson's real personality, the focus that drove him, and the psychic factors that made him Woodson, have passed, or are rapidly passing, from the scene."[171]

In 1991, the *Journal of Negro History* featured two reflections on Woodson. Marion J. Pryde's "My Personal and Family Reminiscences of Dr. Carter G. Woodson" and Willie Leanna Miles's "Dr. Carter G. Woodson as I Recall Him, 1943–1950." A cousin of Woodson's who worked for the Department of Special Education in D.C. public schools, Pryde recalled how in 1920 Woodson visited her family in Washington, D.C. She remembered that Woodson was affectionate toward children, committed to family, ate Thanksgiving and Christmas dinners at her family's home and shared stories and family histories. Once when Woodson visited Pryde's family on Christmas, he arrived "with his arms full of gifts. For each child he had wrapped a book in white tissue paper and tied it with a red ribbon. Each book was based on Negro history." Woodson also helped Pryde with her homework. "He loved teaching and loved young people," Pryde avowed. "On warms days the children of his neighborhood liked to gather on his front steps and listen to his stories, his advice, and to enjoy an ice cream cone that came at the close of the hour." She concluded: "His gifts of inspiration, his devotion to family, his love for his people and his lighting the torch which blazed the path for other historians are, however, gifts to which we shall be ever heirs—gifts we always will treasure and revere."[172]

In her 1991 *Journal of Negro History* recollection, Willie Leanna Miles, who worked with Woodson from 1943 until 1950, provided very revealing descriptions of Woodson's office-home and Woodson's personality. In offering her "bird's-eye view" of her "memories of the man and his life," Miles described the Carter G. Woodson Home. Miles reconstructed a floor plan of the four levels of Woodson's home and concluded that Woodson, the somewhat private, "aloof" and "lonely man," shared in the comforts of his home stories of his past with his visitors, co-workers and employees. In 1998, the *Journal of Negro History* published its last major recollection on Woodson, the reflections of Charles H. Wesley from 1975 that largely reiterate what he said about his elder in essays that he wrote in the 1950s and 1960s.

On September 29, 2006, at ASNLH's ninety-first annual convention in Atlanta, Georgia, sociologist Adelaide M. Cromwell and historian

John Hope Franklin imparted valuable insights into Woodson's character. In 2007, ASNLH released a DVD featuring these recollections, *Reflections on Carter G. Woodson*. Born and raised in Washington, D.C., Cromwell, who met Woodson on several occasions, labeled him "a very paradoxical person." She also discussed his progressive views of Africa and his sensitivity toward the "average person."

Franklin's reminiscences were derived from his relationship with Woodson, "the patron saint of the whole area of minority history in the United States," in his words, from the fall of 1936 until the early spring of 1950. Franklin recalled how he, at age twenty-one, first met Woodson in 1936 at the ASNLH annual meeting in Petersburg, Virginia, at Virginia State College. Franklin was especially impressed with the commitment of Woodson and his "small staff," the presence of white scholars (at least a half dozen) at this meeting, the active participation of black elementary and high school teachers, the contributions of "Woodson's Boys" and the overall welcoming and supportive intellectual and social atmosphere. Franklin described his first meeting with Woodson, noting that Woodson with his "big heart" welcomed him into the ranks of the association with open arms. He commented that Woodson was all about "business," "knew everything," never held a conference at a HBCU during a "football weekend" and planned the conference largely by himself. Franklin was in awe with how Woodson was "in every way so dedicated" to the dissemination of African American history with "no surrender of scholarship." As others have said, Franklin emphasized that Woodson "*was* the Association."

This 1936 meeting profoundly changed Franklin; it marked a significant turning point in his life. He was "in a cloud" when he shared a meal and conversation with Mary McLeod Bethune, Rayford W. Logan and others. While at this conference, Franklin received a telegram indicating that his mother was in critical condition and that he needed to return to Tulsa, Oklahoma, immediately. After he made the long journey from Virginia to Oklahoma, his mother died on November 1, 1936. Franklin recalled how before he left Virginia, he informed Woodson what had happened. Franklin said that Woodson comforted him and pulled out his wallet to give him money for his fare. Franklin retold this story in his autobiography, *Mirror to America: The Autobiography of John Hope Franklin* (2005), as well: "When I found him [Woodson], I told him why I was rushing away, at which point he put an arm around me, expressed his concern, and asked if I needed any money." This conference, in

Franklin's words, represented a "remarkable transforming experience of my life." From that point on, he said that he had two fathers: Buck Colbert Franklin and Carter G. Woodson.

Between 1936 and 1950, Franklin underscored that he developed a close relationship with Woodson, corresponding with him and visiting in Washington, D.C., regularly. Franklin attested that Woodson helped him with his research, encouraging and supporting him in a variety of ways. In one of their conversations, Franklin asked Woodson why he wrote so many book reviews for the *Journal of Negro History*. Woodson replied that he assumed this responsibility out of necessity. The journal, he revealed, received many books to review from many presses on a regular basis, and Woodson would send out the books to be reviewed and often those to whom he sent the books would not provide him with reviews in a timely manner. Woodson, Franklin recalled, was not happy with his colleagues who were too busy teaching and researching. "They don't read and they don't write," Woodson retorted to Franklin. When Franklin was commissioned to write *From Slavery to Freedom* in 1945, he was warned by others in the ASNLH that Woodson would view this project as work that would compete with *The Negro in Our History* (first published in 1922 and, by 1947, in its ninth edition). Franklin avowed that, to the contrary, Woodson was fully supportive of Franklin's book, noting that in 1947, Woodson placed him on the editorial board of the *Journal of Negro History*.

Franklin also shared how Woodson was supportive of his research on George Washington Williams. In fact, Woodson encouraged Franklin to write a biography of Williams. When Franklin first discovered Williams's 1882 *History of the Negro Race*, he asked Woodson who Williams was. Woodson responded: "He was quite a scholar, an important person" and then instructed Franklin to write a paper on his life and work. Woodson assigned Franklin to a panel in the ASNLH program in 1945 to deliver a paper on Williams. In January 1946, Franklin's paper was published as an article in the *Journal of Negro History*. This article marked the beginnings of a larger work that took forty years to complete, Franklin's second opus, *George Washington Williams: A Biography* (1985), which was the runner-up for the Pulitzer Prize for History. Franklin concluded his "deeply, deeply personal" firsthand account with gratitude and humility: "I am proud to stand here and say were it not for Carter Godwin Woodson before me, I would not be here either." Though uncritical, Franklin's 2006 recollections are crucial because there are very few people who knew Woodson personally who were still living during the new millennium.

Franklin's talk will probably remain the most detailed account of Woodson produced since the early 1990s. I strongly recommend the ASNLH's DVD *Reflections on Carter G. Woodson*, especially because of John Hope Franklin's heartfelt testimonies.

What follows are extensive recollections of Woodson by Lorenzo J. Greene and Woodson's cousin Marion J. Pryde. Together, these detailed remembrances reveal intriguing elements of Woodson's personality.

RECOLLECTIONS FROM LORENZO JOHNSTON GREENE (CIRCA 1965, MID-1970S, 1985)

"Dr. Carter G. Woodson: The Man as I Knew Him"

It is virtually impossible to evaluate a personality as intricate as that of Dr. Woodson. Although for twenty-years, I was closely associated directly or indirectly with Dr. Woodson, I cannot say that I really knew the man. I doubt seriously whether anyone save a few very intimate persons such as Dr. John W. Davis, Mrs. Mary McLeod Bethune, or Attorney Louis Mehlinger really knew him. To most persons, Dr. Woodson wrapped himself in a seemingly forbidding exterior which, effectively repelled any effort to penetrate to his inner self. Few, if any, took the liberty to call him "Carter." To intimate associate or casual acquaintance alike he was Dr. Woodson. *During all the years I knew Dr. Woodson, I only heard one person address him familiarly as "Carter"...This privileged individual was Mrs. Bethune.*

It is not too much to say that my association with Dr. Woodson changed the entire course of my life...Dr. Woodson was a many-sided man. To you, who did not know him, he was robust, healthy-looking, light-brown in color, of somewhat more than average height, with thin tightly-pursed lips. He often wore a scowling, condescending expression on his face. At other times, his face would light up in a smile with a roughish twinkle in his eyes. His eyesight was good, but he wore gold rimmed glasses for reading. When I went to work with him he was fifty-three. His browning hair was thinning about the temples, his head balding, and his lower lip protruded at times beyond the upper one, giving him an aspect of scorn or determination...

Personally, Dr. Woodson had many admirable traits. He was an indefatigable worker. Besides writing and editing books, turning out scores of articles, founding [and] editing the Journal of Negro History *and later the* Negro History Bulletin, *Woodson maintained a grueling schedule of speaking engagements throughout the country...Also, he had the knack of gripping and holding his audience through his crusading zeal, and his ability to interlay his abundant facts with timely anecdotes. He both informed and entertained his audience. Speaking without notes, he employed his vast arsenal of facts to explode myths, stereotypes, rationalizations, falsehoods, omissions, and racial bias concerning the Negro…Dr. Woodson always spoke at some length—an hour or longer, yet he never failed to receive a prolonged ovation from his audience—whether mixed or not—starving for authoritative information to controvert the traditional picture of the Negro.*

In his own way, Woodson also had the ability to inspire loyalty in his co-workers. In my opinion, however, this loyalty was to the cause and not to the man. Many admired *Woodson, but few could* love *him. It was certainly so with me. Woodson had little consideration for the feelings of his co-workers. On several occasions when he cruelly hurt me, I remained faithful to him but only because of the movement which he personified.*

The devotion which Woodson stimulated in his subordinates stemmed from his whole-hearted dedication to Negro history and the tremendous personal sacrifices which he made to carry on the work. He drove himself mercilessly, regularly working sixteen to eighteen hours a day. When I asked him how he did it, he chuckled and replied that laboring in the coal mines of West Virginia had given him the physical energy to carry on.

Woodson was no snob, no work was too menial for him. He cooked his own breakfast, generally of cereal, bacon, eggs, toast, and coffee in a kitchen to the rear of his office. Many a morning the delicious tell-tale aroma of frying bacon would greet my nostrils as I entered the building…

You cannot imagine how very humble I felt before this man who, despite his stature as a historian, would cook, wash dishes, sweep and scrub floors, fire the furnace, take out ashes; in fact, do everything from janitor and charwoman to author, lecturer, and editor. And all for the cause. *Much as I desired to be an integral part of the Association and share in all its responsibilities, whatever their nature, I could not persuade Woodson to let me perform duties other than those for which he employed me. The only opportunity I had to do so was when he was out of town.*

But such occasions were rare. Regularly Woodson wrapped and packed books, prepared them for shipment and carried them or letters to the main Post Office. It was a common sight, winter or summer, in fair or foul weather, for him to leave the office between ten-thirty and midnight with a mail bag crammed with books or letters on his way to the Post Office. Never once did he ask me to do so, or even to help him. If I wrapped books, it was because I volunteered, or he was out of town…

Dr. Woodson, also was a staunch advocate of physical fitness. He never bought a car for himself in order to exercise by walking. Although he did not play golf or tennis, probably because he believed he could not spare the time to do so, he walked where and whenever possible, whether to church, the Post Office, Library of Congress, or to the home where he ate dinner, no matter how inclement the weather. He also advised me to do the same, excellent advice which I honored in the breach...

Woodson had a sense of humor that was both delightful and sardonic...One October night I came out of a theatre on "U" street with a young woman. While inside, the weather had turned unexpectedly cold and a brisk wind was blowing. Whom should I meet, muffled up in his topcoat, but Dr. Woodson. Seeing me without a coat and obviously cold, Woodson, ignoring the young lady, blurted out: "Mr. Greene, you had better put on your topcoat, if you have one." *For some time, Woodson had helped support his brother, Robert, who made frequent demands on him for money. One day, he sent Woodson an urgent telegram asking for help. "Save me Carter," it read, "or I am lost." Woodson wired back, "Can't save you, Robert, I am already lost."*

Along with his sense of humor, Woodson could be kind, considerate, even fatherly. One Christmas when his sisters sent him a fruit cake, Woodson gave it to me saying: "Take it Mr. Greene, you are away from home." When the office girls asked to be paid before Christmas, Woodson, after cautioning them they would probably be broke by New Year's Day, gave them their checks on December 20, so they might do their Christmas shopping.

At times he manifested a paternal interest in me, constantly advising me to safeguard my health in general. Particularly did he admonish me to eat properly, and exercise especially by walking. Dr. Woodson generally enjoyed good health. I never knew him to miss a day from the office because of illness...

Woodson possessed a phenomenal memory. He amazed me by the way he remembered the names of persons, often identifying them with their places of residence, work, or some relative...

For all his hectic existence, Dr. Woodson lived a lonely life. Virtually all his time and energy he devoted to the Association. You probably know he never married. When I asked why, his stock answer was that he had been in love once, had been jilted, and subsequently had followed the woman around like a little "fice" dog. She married someone else. To my knowledge, he did manifest some interest in a comely-widow from West Virginia, but nothing came of it...Woodson told me many times that marriage would interfere with his life's work, Negro history, to which he was dedicated. True or not, his attitude, I am sure, influenced my own relatively late marriage.

Dr. Woodson loved children, I have seen him talk to elementary pupils and regale them with some of the beautiful and interesting African myths which he had collected and published...Their little faces would light up with joy, and their evident happiness affected Dr. Woodson. As he talked to them, it seemed that the years fell away from him. His countenance lighted up; the scowl disappeared, his face broke into smiles and often he laughed heartily. In fact, he appeared positively human. As I watched, my heart went out for him, for I believed that Woodson saw in these children the offspring which, he so longed for but had denied himself because of his selfless dedication to the work of the Association.

And yet Woodson did have children. Married to the Association, his offspring were not only the numerous books, scholarly papers, and other achievements which he had wrought, but far more important were his children unrelated by blood—his boys as he called us—Now Dr. Wesley, Dr. Reddick, Dr. A.A. Taylor, Dr. Luther Porter Jackson, Dr. Franklin and humble self, Dr. W. Sherman Savage, Dr. Benjamin Quarles. Although we were his pride, for it was his torch that had ignited us, he was never overgenerous in his praise, yet he knew that he could always count on us...Although frequently hurt, disillusioned, and hating the things that Woodson did, nevertheless, we always decided that the cause was bigger than the man and remained loyal to the Association...

Although we feuded, and all too often I would leave, telling him I never wanted to see him again, I always returned. My appreciation of the man is expressed by this concluding anecdote: At an Annual Meeting of the Association held in Washington, D.C. Dr. Mordecai Johnson, President of Howard University and one of America's foremost orators, was the main speaker at the public meeting. After he had brought his audience to its feet following an eloquent eulogy of Dr. Woodson's historical contributions, I later confided in my diary that if at that moment I had the choice of being President of the United States or Dr. Woodson, my decision unhesitatingly would have been Carter G. Woodson...

Dr. Woodson was modest regarding his achievements. Realizing his greatness and his vast contribution to historiography which he was making, I asked him one day who would write his biography. "No one," he replied with a twinkle in his eye, "because there would be nothing to write about"...

Woodson's views on religion were not orthodox. Whether he believed in a hereafter or not, I cannot say. Although he attended church, I do not know whether he did so regularly. He held that religion should enable a man to live that he might be at peace with his own conscience. True religion, he went on, was not in words but in the guidance of one's life by lofty principles, utter lack of vindictiveness, and in service rendered to one's fellowman. Then he impressed upon me the importance of living in accordance to the golden rule. "Never," he counseled, "and this should be taken seriously by you—do anything that you would not have someone do to you." I told him that this was the creed by which I tried to live.

Nevertheless he believed in retributive justice. No man, he admonished me, can sin with impunity without reaping the reward of his folly...

In all fairness to Dr. Woodson, he was not unmindful of his faults which made it difficult for persons to work with him. Just before I accepted the position of research assistant to him, he volunteered, "I suppose you have heard, Mr. Greene, that I am eccentric, that I do things in fits and starts." Not only had I been told, but had experienced such. However, my only reply was that all I desired was to know what my job was. I would carry on. He did not answer...For all his weaknesses, and what man does not have them, Woodson must remain one of the greatest figures in Twentieth Century American historiography. His place in history is assured...As Dr. Woodson so often said, "Know the truth and the truth shall set you free."

RECOLLECTIONS FROM MARION J. PRYDE (1991)

"My Personal and Family Reminiscences of Dr. Carter Godwin Woodson"

It was a bright fall day back in 1920, I believe, that my mother announced that her cousin, Carter Woodson, was coming to see us. She dressed us in our Sunday clothes, reminded us of good manners and impressed all six children of the fact that our visitor was a world traveler and a teacher in a high school. My oldest sister, Beatrice, filled me with awe when she observed that Cousin Carter Woodson had been to the Holy Lands. I was about nine years old at the time with a poor sense of geography. "I thought the Holy Lands were in heaven," I protested. I had learned in Sunday School that Jesus Christ lived in the Holy Lands. I knew He was in heaven. Sister Bea cleared the matter up just as our guest arrived.

Each child was lined up according to age and presented to our august relative. One thing that stood out in my mind was how warmly Cousin Carter Woodson greeted my baby sister, Ursula. True, she was a cute little four-year-old with bright eyes, black curls, framing a dimpled face and a friendly disposition. I was not prepared after the pleasant nod he had afforded the rest of us, to see him smile broadly, lean forward in his chair and extend a hand of greeting so cordial that I thought he might lift her onto his lap...

At the close of the visit Dr. Woodson observed that we were his closest relatives in Washington. Whereupon my mother invited him to Thanksgiving dinner, an offer he eagerly accepted. From that time on whenever he was in Washington, Dr. Woodson came to have Christmas and Thanksgiving dinners with us.

Dr. Woodson did the talking. We did the admiring and the listening...At Christmas time we were delighted to open the door to a smiling Cousin Woodson with his arms full of gifts. For each child he had wrapped a book in white tissue paper and tied it with red ribbon. Each book was based on Negro history—one that he had written or one published by his firm, The Associated Publishers, Inc. Over the years he created for us a valuable library of first editions in Black History...

My mother, whose name was Anne Eliza, did not care for her given name at all. She insisted that all her nieces and nephews call her "Auntie" until she learned from her illustrious cousin that she had been named for his mother, Anne Eliza Woodson.

As I reflect upon the past, certain incidents come to mind like tiny vignettes. My eldest sister, Beatrice, who was in high school, forgot to carry her lunch to school one day. Mama called the school and asked Dr. Woodson to see that Bea got something to eat. He gave my sister fifty cents—a half dollar! What a gift! She was able to buy lunch on two days.

My eldest brother, Charles, was a "live wire." He was rebellious and dropped out of high school to make money. He got a job as a waiter on a train. As he went about his chores he spotted Dr. Woodson in the dining car. He tried his best to ignore a voice calling out imperiously "Young man—young man." The head waiter directed my brother's attention to the diner who questioned, "Aren't you Eliza Jackson's boy? Why aren't you in school?" My brother eventually returned to high school to earn his diploma.

One Thanksgiving Day after dinner I dropped the fact that I was beginning to study French. Dr. Woodson sent me for my textbook and proceeded to help me with my homework. He loved teaching and he loved young people. He brought his niece, Jennie Woodson, to Washington and enrolled her in Nannie Helen Burroughs' School. He also brought a nephew, Robert, by the house to meet us...

Upon returning from a trip to Africa, Dr. Woodson dropped by to deliver books to Bea and to me. For Ursula he had a beautiful tooled leather bag. He said she would prefer it to a book. (So would I, but I never admitted it.) I learned later that Dr. Woodson had proposed marriage to a young lady, but she refused because she did not want to go to the Philippines where he was to teach. That lady's name was Ursula.

Mama tried to play match-maker, so anxious was she to have her bachelor cousin lead a full life. When Dr. Clinton Barnett's widow, Clara, came to Washington, dinner at our house for the two was the first order of business. Dr. Woodson who had visited the Barnetts at Lakin was happy to renew their relationship. He took her to dinner, to the movies and the two enjoyed many happy hours reminiscing about their Virginia heritage. But no commitment was forthcoming. Of Woodson, it was said that he was wedded to his work and his books were his children.

At Christmas time he continued his gifts of books to the children. For mama, however, he brought a large box of chocolates and for dad, in later years, he brought a tie...

It was at a family dinner that he first asked my sister and me to write stories for the [Negro History] Bulletin. He had a wealth of information that he wanted published for children but his style, he explained, was too formal and advanced for youngsters he wished to reach. He was pleased with our stories and elated when Bea wrote a play, "The Thrilling Escape of William and Ellen Craft"...

My last recollection of this kind and eminent family man was at the Christmas dinner before his death. He brought books for my son, Paul, Jr. and for my daughter, Marilyn. I now appreciated the importance of the man and asked that he auto-graph my children's books. He was hesitant, saying that he was reluctant to do so because he was not the author. He bowed to my insistence, however, for which I am grateful. They were the last of his Christmas gifts.

EPILOGUE

char·ac·ter *(kar'ək ter)* **n.**, *the mental and moral qualities distinctive to an individual…the quality of being individual, typically in an interesting or unusual way, strength and originality in a person's nature.*
hagi·og·ra·phy *(hag´ē äl'ə fē)* **n.**, *biography of a saint, biography revering its subject.*
iden·ti·ty *(īden'tə tē)* **n.**, *the fact of being who or what a person or thing is… the characteristics determining this.*
per·son·al·ity *(pʉr´sə nal'ə tē)* **n.**, *the combination of characteristics or qualities that form an individual's distinctive character…qualities that make someone interesting or popular.*

Deciphering historical figures' identities, characters and personalities can be a challenging endeavor, especially if the particular individual did not leave behind extensive personal records. Fortunately, Woodson wrote a lot. Equally important, as indicated in the previous chapter, more than a few of his co-workers who knew him intimately reflected on who they perceived him to be. Collectively, these reminiscences help us reconstruct Woodson's "intricate" personality. There are enough sources to reconstruct the basic features of Woodson's character. Vacillating between Type A and Type B personalities, Woodson was complex and simple.

If we were forced to characterize Woodson based on photos, we would perhaps tend to conclude that he was stern. At the same time, there are a few photos of the ASNLH founder smiling and surrounded by children. Besides the fact that he was described as being physically fit by several of his co-workers, we have only a few physical descriptions of Woodson. W. Montague Cobb recollected: "His erect carriage, broad shoulders and sturdy chest, developed during his days in the coalmines of West Virginia, indicated the rugged strength that carried him through his long career." In 1991, Willie Leanna Miles recounted: "Dr. Woodson had penetrating eyes, thin lips, and a very rigid posture. He was light-skinned, stood about 5 feet eight inches tall, wore a size 10 shoe, size 15½ x 24 shirt and weighed about 175 pounds. Bear in mind, Dr. Woodson was in his 68th year when I met him."

In 1921, Swiss psychiatrist and founder of analytical psychology Carl Jung published his classic *Psychological Types* in which he explored, among other elements, the concept of personality types, referring to the psychological classifications of different types of individuals. At one point, Jung identified eight personality types. Major theories pertaining to personality types—including the Enneagram of Personality, the Four Temperaments, Humorism, the Keirsey Temperament Theory, Type A and Type B Personality Theory and the Myers-Briggs Type Indicator— were inspired by Jung's ideas. Psychologists who ascribed to these theories would have certainly come up with a host of interesting conclusions regarding Woodson's personality. In the twenty-first century, a significant group of psychologists have critiqued these limiting personality type theories, instead offering other models that focus on more diversely conceptualized and fluid personality traits. Among those popular models is the Big Five Personality Traits (openness, conscientiousness, extraversion, agreeableness and neuroticism). These traits could perhaps serve as useful points of departure to analyze Woodson.

In describing Woodson's personality, I define personality traits as people's behavioral tendencies or distinguishing qualities or characteristics. "In other words, this means that personality traits are the distinguishing characteristics that make you 'you.' Personality traits are the unique set of characteristics and qualities that only you possess. While a lot of people might have similar personality traits, each person combines these traits in a different way, to create one unique, irreplaceable conglomeration of traits that make up their individual personality."[173]

While I do not pretend to be well versed in psychology or personality trait theory, in what follows I summarize and highlight key aspects of Woodson's personality traits with a list of adjectives and descriptors in bold print. This is meant to serve as a quick reference guide for describing Woodson's personality.

Afrocentric—He placed Africa at the center of many of his analyses of world history. He wrote a collection of books and numerous book reviews and essays on African history and culture, especially for children. Woodson highlighted the Africanity and blackness of ancient Egypt and Africa; celebrated the civilizations of Ghana, Songhai, Mali, Dahomey and Timbuktu; and declared that Ra Nehesi and Nefertari were "full blooded Negroes" and that Ethiopia was "a highly civilized Negro land." During the Harlem Renaissance, Woodson pronounced: "At no time did the Negroes fail to figure conspicuously in the civilization of Egypt." In 1921, Woodson also argued that scholars had not yet engaged in "intensive" studies "of the institutions of the peoples of the interior of Africa." In defending black America's African origins, Woodson belittled white America's early European background. Woodson's rhetoric is similar to the blatant critiques of European culture and intellectual thought offered by outspoken modern Afrocentric Nile Valley thinkers.

ambitious—Woodson set very high expectations for what he and the ASNLH could accomplish. Woodson possessed a strong desire and determination to succeed in legitimizing and popularizing black history. He was especially ambitious when it came to fundraising efforts. In 1934, he even requested $2 million from Rockefeller's General Education Board in order to build what he called an Institute of Black Culture.

cantankerous—This is a term that has been used to describe Woodson on more than a few occasions. His cantankerousness can be best explained by the hard life that he lived and the sacrifices that he made on a daily basis.

committed—From the founding of the ASNLH in 1915 until his death, Woodson expressed complete dedication and loyalty to the study and popularization of black history. Thus, he is the sole holder of the title the "Father of Black History." Woodson was recognized for his commitment to black history during his lifetime. In the 1940s, several people called him "the father of Negro history."[174]

driven—He was driven by the desire to popularize and legitimize black history. He routinely referred to the early black history movement as a "life-and-death struggle." His drive was remarkable. He worked incessantly. His drive was contagious.

family oriented—Woodson never married (he was married to his work), yet he was close to his relatives. He took care of several relatives during his life; left them some money in his will; owned a home in Huntington,

West Virginia, that was used by his family; and visited his parents, especially his mother, until they died. Not only did he support his family members who were struggling, but he regularly visited his family during the holidays. His extended family was certainly the ASNLH membership and especially those on the executive council, his "Boys," his neighbors and his church brethren and sisters.

focused—He was focused on black history, morning, noon and night. Black history was the center of his interests, activities and life.

forward thinking—He was always thinking ahead. He perceived his actions as being directly linked to the future, believing that his efforts were laying the foundations for the future development of the study and popularization of black history. For instance, he remarked that he wanted Negro History Week to develop into Negro History Year. He looked forward to the day when black history would be integrated into American educational institutions.

frugal—Woodson was sparring and economical in regard to money. He did not waste money, as he indicated in his explanation for why he never married. He spent little money on himself (except when vacationing in places like Paris, France). Instead, he invested everything into the ASNLH and the early black history movement. Unlike many of today's black public intellectuals, Woodson did not reap profits from black history. He performed most of the maintenance to his home. He paid his employees in cash, and many of the secretaries complained about their wages.

generous (especially to children)—He may have guarded his time "like a soldier," but he often shared his expertise with and mentored numerous younger scholars. Woodson devoted a great deal of time to producing juvenile literature. He also routinely spoke at elementary and high schools and enlisted his ASNLH co-workers to do the same. He also ultimately created Negro History Week for children. Despite the seemingly permanent frown on his face, many who knew him said that there was a soft spot for children in his heart. According to the *Afro-American* (Washington), "Dr. Woodson was never happier than when surrounded by children who idolized him." Lorenzo J. Greene similarly observed: "Dr. Woodson loved children, I have seen him talk to elementary pupils and regale them with some of the beautiful and interesting African myths which he had collected and published…Their little faces would light up with joy, and their evident happiness affected Dr. Woodson. As he talked to them, it seemed that the years fell away from him. His countenance lighted up; the scowl disappeared, his face broke into smiles and often he laughed heartily." The children who lived near Woodson's "office home" certainly welcomed Woodson. He shared historical stories and African folktales with them, and he "enjoyed taking little treats of candy to the neighborhood children around 9th Street, or buying them ice cream." Woodson also corresponded with children and their letters were often shared with the recipients' entire class.

grass roots oriented—Woodson, who came from a poor background, possessed a commitment to uplifting the black masses. In "The Educated Negro Leaves the Masses," (Chapter 6 in *The Mis-Education of the Negro*), Woodson chastised black leaders who were not grass roots in orientation. He embraced this philosophy throughout his life.

hardworking—All of Woodson's close co-workers commented on Woodson's herculean work ethic. It was widely known that he regularly worked eighteen hours per day. Charles H. Wesley commented that Woodson had a "Spartan-like existence." After his death, members of the executive council unanimously agreed that he did the work of four or more men. As underscored in a "Biographical Sketch" in the *Negro History Bulletin*, "The most remarkable feature of the Association is that it was pretty much of a 'one man job.'" His hard work ethic certainly stemmed back to his early years.

humble—Woodson was modest in his accomplishments. He never wrote an autobiography and strongly discouraged his "Boys" from publishing assessments of his accomplishments while he was still living. While black newspapers praised the work of Woodson, sessions at the ASNLH annual meetings were not devoted to the accomplishments of their founder. He ran the ASNLH in the manner that he wanted to, but he also delegated responsibility to those who were "willing to sacrifice." Woodson also credited those who contributed to the early black history movement with various awards that were given out annually.

humorous—Woodson possessed a sarcastic, clever and interesting sense of humor. One of his co-workers said that he could tell jokes "like a chain smoker." More than a few of his co-workers recalled his wittiness. When reading *The Mis-Education of the Negro* and many of Woodson's newspaper essays and columns, it is hard not to smile or laugh. Woodson's persona and image was so serious that when he joked, it was probably surprising.

iconoclastic—Woodson was an iconoclast, one who directly challenged conventionally cherished beliefs, institutions and ideas. This is perhaps best epitomized in *The Mis-Education of the Negro*, an all out indictment of "highly-educated Negroes."

independent—According to Woodson's biographers, Woodson was fiercely independent when it came to running the association. While he had many co-workers and delegated responsibilities to them, he often acted free from outside control, not depending on anyone else's authority. In 1916, for instance, he launched the first volume of the *Journal of Negro History* without the consent of the executive council. It was his independent spirit that in part influenced him to sever ties from white philanthropists during the early 1930s. In terms of his thought, he was not influenced by his contemporaries, and he did not rely on other historians' ideas in framing his historical interpretations. He also encouraged independent thought in others. In terms of politics, he was independent, critiquing both of the major political parties. While the books published by the Associated Publishers, Inc., and the journal and the *Bulletin* were printed outside of the "national office," Woodson did not pay printers to produce duplicate letters. The staff typed these letters out, as Willie Leanna Miles recalled.

inspirational—In his own way, Woodson had the ability to animate and urge others to join the early black history movement. In a 1950 *Negro History Bulletin* essay, "Dr. Carter G. Woodson, Inspirer and Benefactor of Young Scholars," Alrutheus A. Taylor captured Woodson's ability to inspire others. In 1949, a black high school teacher, Carrie E. Johnson, wrote to Woodson: "Must say that your work has been my greatest inspiration in making me want to devote all of my time to the study of my race."

organizer (leader)—As the founder, director and leader of the ASNLH and its various activities, Woodson mobilized teachers, scholars, social activists and others into a structured movement. He coordinated the activities of the association efficiently. Followed by many, he was the principal player in the early black history movement.

outspoken—This term epitomizes Woodson's thought, for he was frank—at times perhaps too much so for many—in declaring his controversial and critical opinions. His outspokenness often got him into some trouble. At the same time, Woodson controlled his outspokenness in the early years of the ASNLH, as demonstrated by his decision not to publish "The Case of the Negro" (1921). By the 1930s, Woodson did not hold his tongue in *The Mis-Education of the Negro* and numerous essays and columns in the *New York Age*, the *Pittsburgh Courier*, the *New York Amsterdam News* and the *Afro-American*.

passionate—Woodson was passionate about black history, driven by the fear that if he did not do his work that African Americans would become "a negligible factor in the thought of the world." This feeling that he had toward black history was caused by a strong and intense set of feelings that most during and after his times could not relate to.

physically fit—According to one of his co-workers, Woodson was a "staunch advocate of physical fitness." He routinely walked around Washington, D.C. According to a "Biographical Sketch" in the *Negro History Bulletin*, "on reaching fifty-five he gave up tennis in favor of walking." Rayford W. Logan noted in 1950: "His robust health and almost Spartan-like life enabled him to continue teaching and writing." Woodson viewed health as being an important issue for the black community. For instance, in 1949, he noted: "We ought to work for better health, even if it takes a National Negro Health Week to help us achieve it."

pioneering—Dubbed the "Father of Black History," Woodson was a scholarly pioneer, among the first to research and develop a new area of knowledge and a reform movement.

practical/pragmatic—One of Woodson's favorite leaders was Booker T. Washington. Though Woodson obviously embraced "higher education," he was also very practical. He wanted to use history, a traditional discipline in U.S. higher academia, to uplift the masses of blacks, especially the youth. The vast majority of Woodson's publications were targeted at the masses and black youth, and he created a host of practical programs to popularize, institutionalize and legitimize black history—namely, the *Negro History Bulletin*, Negro History Week, ASNLH branches and the association's Extension Division and Home Study Department.

progressive—While influenced by "old school" southern ways, Woodson was committed to implementing social change, reform and new ideas. His gender politics were especially progressive for his times, as demonstrated by the central role of the women in the ASNLH's daily operations.

prolific—Between 1915 and the late 1940s, Woodson wrote and published large quantities of scholarship: more than twenty books, a collection of historically scientific journal articles and countless book reviews and newspaper essays and columns.

radical—In 1915, Woodson dubbed himself a "radical." Not only did he interact with many black radicals and sympathize with black socialists and communists, but many of his ideas, actions, rhetoric, style and approaches were radical in nature (e.g., nontraditional and nonconventional, extreme, challenging to the mainstream, counter-normative, sweeping and/or threatening to white American political, economic and cultural systems). Woodson often challenged the conventional racism and Eurocentrism of U.S. academia, popular culture and historical profession; called for drastic changes and reforms in the social order of American society; chastised white America for its collective mistreatment of blacks; and critiqued the normative and widespread worldviews of black middle-class and elite leadership. The tone of Woodson's observations and rhetoric were often bold, iconoclastic and unapologetic.

respectable—Though working class to the core, Woodson embraced notions of Progressive-era black reformers' notions of respectability. Like his professional black counterparts, Woodson believed that it was very important that African Americans present themselves in upstanding manners within white America and within their own communities. He wanted blacks to be regarded by the broader society as being proper. He was respectable in his appearance, clothing and behavior, despite the fact that he challenged many in direct, uncompromising manners.

rigorous—In terms of his scholarship, Woodson was extremely thorough, exhaustive and accurate. He adhered to a strict format and set of beliefs and standards. His scholarship was, for the most part, free from errors, and in a pre-technological era, it is amazing to see how error-free the *Journal of Negro History* was between 1916 until 1950.

serious—Woodson was very thoughtful, at times solemn. Although he joked with his co-workers often with sarcastic humor, in public he spoke sincerely and in earnest. His seriousness carried over to his strictness. Many of his employees testified that he ran the association offices in a very organized fashion and that he had little patience with incompetence.

shaped by racism—Woodson ran the ASNLH from 1915 until 1950, the era of Jim Crow segregation and widespread anti-black thought and behavior. He was a product of this time. His personality traits were significantly influenced by the particular period in which he existed.

stubborn—When he made decisions, Woodson was committed to them. He was not likely to bend his opinion when his mind was set. This is demonstrated with the conflicts that he had with Du Bois, the Phelps-Stokes Fund and the *Encyclopedia Africana*. Woodson possessed a sense of dogged determination not to change his attitude or position on issues of importance to him. Though many of his co-workers were committed to him and his cause, he had his fair share of conflicts with his closest co-workers, such as Lorenzo Johnston Greene, Charles H. Wesley and

Rayford W. Logan. He had especially enduring conflicts with Logan, W.E.B. Du Bois and Benjamin Brawley.

traveled—Woodson was experienced in traveling throughout the United States and the world. Not only did annual ASNLH meetings and lectures take Woodson throughout the States, but he also visited the Philippines, Asia, Europe and Africa. Charles H. Thompson once met him in Paris, France, and was impressed with his knowledge of French culture.

unselfish—Woodson often demanded that the "Talented Tenth" be more unselfish. As he demonstrated throughout his life, he was willing to put the needs and wishes of others before his own. He respected and often celebrated the achievements and contributions of his co-workers, especially black female schoolteachers.

well read—The second African American to earn a PhD in history, Woodson was very intelligent and well read. He read incessantly, as indicated in the hundreds of book reviews that he authored and published in the *Journal of Negro History*. He also read books published throughout Europe. He possessed reading proficiency in more than a few romance languages. There were thousands of books in his "office home."

working class—Before becoming a teacher and professional historian, Woodson belonged to the large group of African Americans who were employed for low wages in manual, agricultural and/or industrial work. The son of former slaves who worked as a sharecropper, manual laborer, garbage collector and coal miner, Woodson maintained his working-class identity throughout his life. He routinely reminded people that he "could do anything" because he was once a coal miner. Mary McLeod Bethune noted: "He was a man of the soil. He grew to young manhood the hard self-taught way."

WOODSON'S LEGACY

Woodson was unquestionably one of the most influential historian-educators that this nation has produced.
—L.D. Reddick, 1953

Inevitably, the active direction of our Association, which our leader has laid down, will pass to other hands—capable and sure because of his guidance. There will be other directors and other presidents. They will build on the foundation laid

and mortared, stone by stone, with his selfless sacrifice and devotion, translated now into the timeless leadership of the truly great.
—*Mary McLeod Bethune, 1950*

It would be impossible for any one to carry out the multitudinous tasks that Dr. Woodson had learned, through the years, to perform with efficiency and dispatch.
—*Rayford W. Logan, 1950*

The sustaining pride and self assurance that he has given us and that he has inoculated in our group as a result of his authentic research is a priceless legacy for all.
—*Residence of the Phyllis Wheatley YWCA, 901 Rhode Island Avenue, Washington, D.C., 1950*

Today in African American culture, Carter G. Woodson is a legend whose legacies are numerous and obvious to those familiar with the study of black history and the black historical enterprise. They include the Association for the Study of African American Life and History; the *Journal of African American History*; National African American History Month; the enduring and often cited ideas he put forward in *The Mis-Education of the Negro*; the Associated Publishers, Inc. (now The ASALH Press); and the Carter G. Woodson Home, NHS.

Woodson's legacy is symbolically evoked on a daily basis today in the titles and names of awards, fellowships, foundations, libraries and archive collections, organizations, black history clubs, institutes and especially elementary, junior high and high schools. In 1953, association member and Shaw Junior High School teacher Albert N.D. Brooks predicted: "It is natural to expect that many schools having a majority of Negro pupils will take the name of Carter G. Woodson." Brooks proceeded to discuss the "first school named after this great benefactor of his race." On March 1, 1953, "in the auditorium of the shining new building in the Cherry Hill section of Baltimore, Maryland, Public School Number 160 was dedicated as the Carter Godwin Woodson School." Brooks praised this elementary school named after Woodson, declaring:

> *Readers of the* BULLETIN *might compare elementary schools in their areas with the Carter G. Woodson School in Baltimore, to see how their schools measure up to standards of adequacy. The Carter G. Woodson School has a principal and assistant principal to supervise the work*

of thirty-odd teachers…Communities that do not provide schools like the Carter G. Woodson School will probably spend greater sums for hospitals, jails and relief.[175]

A year before Baltimore's Carter G. Woodson School was dedicated, educational reformers in Washington, D.C., initiated a Carter G. Woodson Memorial Fund in hopes of improving the educational opportunities for young Washingtonians attending high, vocational, junior high and elementary public schools.[176] While Woodson was still living, at least one organization was named in his honor. In 1945, a group of young blacks in New York organized "the Carter G. Woodson Negro History Club." Under the guidance of the New York Branch of the ASNLH, this organization sought to stimulate interest in black history among youth, in hopes of instigating a "new program" that "would appeal to and interest a larger group." They held meetings monthly, raised money for the association and Woodson addressed the group and a larger interracial audience on April 24, 1949.[177] Schoolteachers and schoolchildren celebrated Woodson during his lifetime.

Woodson was, in many ways, a living legend. He frequently spoke at public African American elementary, junior high and high schools throughout D.C. In the late 1920s, the *Washington Post* reported on speeches that Woodson delivered at Randall Junior High School, Shaw Junior High School and Armstrong Technical School.[178] Beyond the Spingarn Medal that he received in 1926, Woodson was given many honors by the people who benefited from his "mass education movement." For instance, in 1946 in Washington, D.C., the 1,080 students at Charles Young School, who were taught black history from Woodson's books, signed a scroll that they presented to Woodson pledging their commitment to the association's cause. They then performed a one-act "play sketching Dr. Woodson's career." The event was "acclaimed by the local press," including the *Washington Post,* and was quite a celebration.[179] "The Parent-Teacher Association arranged a display of Dr. Woodson's books and of the two magazines he edits."[180] During Woodson's times, the *Negro History Bulletin* also reprinted countless letters from schoolteachers, children and others that eloquently revealed how much Woodson was revered. One black schoolteacher from Chicago, Madeline R. Morgan (who was among the first to dub Woodson the "father of Negro history"), wrote to Woodson in 1945: "I just telephoned a friend of mine, Grace Markwell, who is doing a most unusual and successful educational program in Negro achievements in her all-white community. I mentioned to her that if you should come to Chicago I wanted her to meet you. In the course of our conversation she mentioned that she might be too awed but I assured her that you were most affable and easy with whom to converse."[181]

After hearing him speak to a crowd of two thousand in Chicago in 1940, a local attorney, Edward A. Simmons, wrote to Woodson:

> *It was my never-to-be-forgotten privilege to hear you Sunday evening and to feel the pride of African ancestry well up within me like it never has been aroused before. My feelings seemed to have been typical of all within the hearing of your voice—that sincere voice of yours that at that time seemed to have been the agency of the Spirit.*
>
> *Sometime in the far distant future you will be justly recognized by posterity as the preserver of a great race—by preserving the record of the great deed of that race. Your fame is assured.*[182]

Woodson was aware of his celebrity-like status in the black community and responded with humility. In 1938, Woodson shared the following with *Bulletin* readers:

> *To the office of the Association for the Study of Negro Life and History at 1538 Ninth Street, Northwest, Washington, D.C., have come suggestions for the celebration of Negro History Week beginning February 6, 1938. Some of the suggestions are mainly personal. One of the many coworkers desires to set aside a special day as Douglass Day. Another would do similar honor to Booker T. Washington, and still another would stretch the plan far enough to devote special attention to the Director of the Association. Neither the Association nor its Director believes that he has done anything to merit his being ranked with the great, and it would be a sad disappointment to the staff to have such exercises assume any such insane turn as to give special attention to one of its officers. The Association combats all efforts of this sort.*[183]

At the same time, several years before he died, Woodson did use images of himself as an educational and promotional device for Negro History Week. By 1948, the association had more than two hundred pictures (eight by ten inches) of famous African Americans and important moments in black history that it sold for Negro History Week celebrations. Of the sixteen new pictures that it introduced in January

EPILOGUE

1948 was one described as follows: "Carter Godwin Woodson, founder of Negro History Week, conducts children through a special exhibit at the Peale Museum in Baltimore."[184]

After his death, Woodson would indeed be "ranked with the great." In recognition of Woodson's contributions and lasting ties to Huntington, West Virginia, in 1986, Mayor Robert Nelson created the Carter G. Woodson Foundation and, in 1994, erected a life-size statue of Woodson on Hal Greer Boulevard. Following this, the foundation and the West Virginia Department of Culture and History placed a highway historical marker in honor of Woodson. There is even a public housing apartment complex named in honor of Woodson in Huntington, West Virginia. The Carter G. Woodson Apartments, Project WV 4-12, is located on Eighth Avenue and Hal Greer Boulevard, has twenty three-bedroom units and was built and leased in 1995.

Woodson's *The Mis-Education of the Negro* is one of his most enduring legacies. In it, he unrelentingly critiqued those blacks educated in America's institutions of higher learning. He called on them to sacrifice for the masses of their people. Woodson implored highly educated leaders and teachers to become servants of the people guided by unselfishness:

The servant of the people, unlike the leader, is not on a high horse elevated above the people and trying to carry them to some designated point to which he would like to go for his own advantage. The servant of the people is down among them, living as they live, doing what they do and enjoying what they enjoy. He may be a little better informed than some other members of the group; it may be that he has had some experience that they have not had, but in spite of this advantage he should have more humility than those whom he serves, for we are told that "Whosoever is greatest among you, let him be your servant."[185]

More than 300,000 different copies of this polemic are said to be in print. In the new millennium, many publishers have republished Woodson's classic, including African American Images, Dover Publications, Khalifah's Booksellers and Associates, Africa Tree Press, Book Tree Press, Black Civilization, Classic House Books, Wilder Publications and most recently CreateSpace. In 2007, *The Mis-Education of the Negro* was even made available as an audiobook. In February 2008, Nike released at special events in New York and Los Angeles "Dr. Carter G. Woodson Black History Month Air Force Ones." In the

This statue of Carter G. Woodson (erected in 1994) is located on Hal Greer Boulevard in Huntington, West Virginia. *Courtesy of West Virginia State Archives.*

insole of these shoes is an often-cited quotation from *The Mis-Education of the Negro*, and on the inside of the box, there is a brief tribute to Woodson. Though not made available to the public at large, these kicks were reviewed well by hip-hop generationers.

Several years ago, the online *Carter Magazine* was founded by Datwon Thomas, the former editor in chief of *King* magazine. Paying homage to Woodson, the magazine seeks to be "the voice that bridges history and shapes hip-hop culture." One of the magazine's mottos is "Where History and Hip-Hop Meets" and the "About" page features a collage with photos of a hodge-podge collection of "Carters," namely Alprentice "Bunchy" Carter, Dwayne "Lil' Wayne" Carter, Betty Carter, Carter G. Woodson and Shawn (Jay Z) Carter. Overall, the magazine does an admirable job of meshing hip-hop culture with dimensions of black history, in a similar manner to the much more popular *Vibe* and *The Source*. This symbolic evocation of Woodson could be dismissed as a surface-level expression of hip-hop generationers' historical revivalism. At the same time, Thomas's sampling from Woodson is perhaps as deliberate as Lauryn Hill's was. It is refreshing at one level to see Woodson being memorialized by hip-hop culturalists.

Nevertheless, today we could benefit from revisiting how Woodson implemented the Negro History Weeks of his times, celebrations that were much more practical and effective than the Black History Months of more recent times. We could more effectively transform black history into something practical, accessible and truly interesting and valuable to the masses of black people, especially to the black youth and hip-hop generation. We could achieve great things by meshing Woodson's vision with our current knowledge and advanced state of technology. During the last decade or so, African American History Month (February)—very much like Kwanzaa (December 26 through January 1) and Martin Luther King Jr. Day (the third Monday of January)—has become commercialized and in many ways co-opted by the materialistic and capitalistic ethos of American culture. In many regards, our annual Black History Month celebrations have been transformed into something that Woodson was vehemently opposed to during his times. Routinely in the pages of the *Negro History Bulletin*, Woodson chastised those who sought to exploit Negro History Week. In the first volume of the *Bulletin*, he jestingly proclaimed:

> *This* [Negro History Week] *cannot be done in the usual style of having a few speeches or essays centered around* [sic] *a great character,*

Lauryn Hill live at Tom Brasil in São Paulo, Brazil, in 2007. Hill memorialized Woodson with her album *The Miseducation of Lauryn Hill* (1998). *Photograph by Daigo Oliva, courtesy of Wikimedia Commons.*

or by having a big dinner at which some spell-binder will set forth the virtues of the great, but before he begins to speak the convivial group has become so surfeited with food and drink that neither he nor his hearers know what he has said. Many of our Lincoln-Douglass celebrations are a disgrace to communities in which they are held. Celebrations of this type have become too frequent, and great men thus supposedly honored would rise in condemnation of such conviviality, if they could look down over the battlements from above and observe such performances.[186]

Woodson never wanted Negro History Week to simply be a weeklong celebration during his times or in the future. Simply put, he wanted Negro History Week to become what he called "Negro History Year." In 1940, Woodson proclaimed:

The important and encouraging result is the gradual elimination of Negro History Week, that is, rendering the effort unnecessary in schools where the Negro is studied so thoroughly that special exercises are no longer exceptional...Before all persons concerned with the study of the Negro must be set this goal of studying the Negro throughout the school year, for thirty-six weeks rather than one week...Readers of this periodical [THE NEGRO HISTORY BULLETIN] *who follow the course of study outlined will understand how to make Negro History Week develop into Negro History Year...There is a growing demand for work-books and syllabi with which to facilitate the study of the Negro and thus make Negro History Week Negro History Year.*

BOOKS AUTHORED, EDITED AND COAUTHORED BY CARTER G. WOODSON

The Education of the Negro Prior to 1861: A History of the Education of the Colored People of the United States from the Beginning of Slavery to the Civil War. New York: Putnam's, 1915.

A Century of Negro Migration. Washington, D.C.: ASNLH, 1918.

The History of the Negro Church. Washington, D.C.: Associated Publishers, Inc., 1921.

Fifty Years of Negro Citizenship as Qualified by the United States Supreme Court. Reprint from *Journal of Negro History* 6 (1921).

"The Case of the Negro." 1921. Reprint, Daryl Michael Scott, ed., *Carter G. Woodson's Appeal*. Washington, DC: ASALH Press, 2008.

Early Negro Education in West Virginia. West Virginia State College, 1921.

The Negro in Our History. Washington, D.C.: Associated Publishers, Inc., 1922.

Free Negro Owners of Slaves in the United States in 1830: Together with Absentee Ownership of Slaves in the United States in 1830 (editor). Washington, D.C.: ASNLH, 1924.

Free Negro Heads of Families in the United States in 1830: Together with a Brief Treatment of the Free Negro. Washington, D.C.: ASNLH, 1925.

Negro Orators and their Orations (editor). Washington, D.C.: Associated Publishers, Inc., 1926.

Ten Years of Collecting and Publishing the Records of the Negro. Washington, D.C.: ASNLH, 1926.

The Mind of the Negro as Reflected in Letters Written During the Crisis, 1800–1860 (editor). Washington, D.C.: ASNLH, 1926.

Negro Makers of History. Washington, D.C.: Associated Publishers, Inc., 1928.

African Myths Together with Proverbs: A Supplementary Reader Composed of Folk Tales from Various Parts of Africa. Washington, D.C.: Associated Publishers, Inc., 1928.

The Negro as Businessman (joint author with John H. Harmon Jr. and Arnett J. Lindsay). Washington, D.C.: Associated Publishers, Inc., 1929.

The Negro Wage Earner (joint author with Lorenzo J. Greene). Washington, D.C.: ASNLH, 1930.

The Rural Negro. Washington, D.C.: ASNLH, 1930.

The Mis-Education of the Negro. Washington, D.C.: Associated Publishers, Inc., 1933.

The Negro Professional Man and the Community: With Special Emphasis on the Physician and the Lawyer. Washington, D.C.: ASNLH, 1934.

The Story of the Negro Retold. Washington, D.C.: Associated Publishers, Inc., 1935.

The African Background Outlined. Washington, D.C.: ASNLH, 1936.

African Heroes and Heroines. Washington, D.C.: Associated Publishers, Inc., 1939.

The Works of Frances J. Grimké (editor). Washington, D.C.: Associated Publishers, Inc., 1942.

CHRONOLOGY

1875: Carter Godwin Woodson is born to former slaves James Henry and Anne Eliza (Riddle) Woodson in New Canton, Virginia, in Buckingham County on December 19.

1877: The end of Reconstruction with the Compromise of 1877 and the beginning of what historian Rayford W. Logan termed "the Nadir" period of the African American experience that lasted until the early twentieth century.

1882: George Washington Williams's *History of the Negro Race in America from 1619 to 1880*, the first major scholarly black history text, is published.

1892: Leaves Buckingham County for West Virginia to work on the railroad and then in the coal mines, where, in Fayette County, he meets black Civil War veteran Olivier Jones, who introduces him to the scholarship of amateur black historians.

1893: Woodson's family move to Huntington, West Virginia.

1894: At age nineteen, Woodson "learned the fundamentals of reading, writing, and arithmetic."

1895: Woodson moves to Huntington, West Virginia, to live with his parents. He attends high school. W.E.B. Du Bois becomes the first African American to earn a PhD in history (at Harvard).

1898–1900: Works as a teacher in Winona, West Virginia.

1903: Graduates from Berea College. Begins working under the auspices of the U.S. War Department in the Philippines.

1907: Travels to Africa, Asia and Europe; attends the Sorbonne in Paris, France; and from October through December attends the University of Chicago as a full-time graduate student.

1908: Receives a master's degree in history, romance languages and literature from the University of Chicago (master's thesis: "The German Policy of France in the War of Austrian Succession").

1908–09: Attends Harvard University as a PhD candidate in history, studying American and European history.

1909–11: Teaches at Armstrong Manual Training High School in Washington, D.C.

1910: Submits the first draft of his PhD dissertation.

1911–17: Teaches French, Spanish, English and history at M Street School (Dunbar High School) in Washington, D.C.

1911: Submits the revised version of his dissertation and participated on the Committee of 200. Becomes founding member of Washington, D.C. NAACP branch.

1912: Successfully defends and completes PhD dissertation, "The Disruption of Virginia."

1914: A total of fourteen blacks have earned PhD degrees by this year.

1915: Woodson publishes his first monograph, *The Education of the Negro Prior to 1861: A History of the Education of the Colored People of the United*

States from the Beginning of Slavery to the Civil War (New York: Putnam's). On September 9, Woodson co-founds the Association for the Study of Negro Life and History (ASNLH) in Chicago with George Cleveland Hall, James E. Stamps and Alexander L. Jackson.

1916: Launches the first issue of the *Journal of Negro History*. Publishes two articles in the journal's first volume, "The Negroes of Cincinnati Prior to the Civil War" and "Freedom and Slavery in Appalachian America."

1917: The first biennial meeting of the ASNLH is held in Washington, D.C. Woodson gives more than $1,000 of his own money to support the *Journal of Negro History* and reorganizes the association's leadership.

1918–19: Serves as principal of Armstrong Manual Training School in Washington, D.C.

1919: Woodson employs J.E. Ormes as a field agent to help increase ASNLH membership, sell books and subscriptions to the *Journal of Negro History* and organize Negro History Clubs. During "The Red Summer," more than twenty-five major race riots sweep through U.S. cities. Woodson is in Washington, D.C., during the July 20 race riot there. He provides an affidavit for this riot.

1919–20: Serves as dean of the School of Liberal Arts at Howard University in Washington, D.C.; introduces the study of black history and graduate studies in history at Howard.

1920: Joins the Friends of Negro Freedom; serves as dean of West Virginia Collegiate Institute (later West Virginia State College, now West Virginia State University).

1921: Founds the Associated Publishers, Inc.; receives grant from the Carnegie Institution; writes "The Case of the Negro."

1922: In February, the Laura Spelman Rockefeller Foundation awards Woodson $25,000. On July 18, Woodson purchases the three-story, Victorian-style brick row house on Lot 819 in Square 365 at 1538 Ninth Street, Northwest. Participates in the Washington, D.C. NAACP Branch's silent parade against lynching in June.

1923: Elizabeth Ross Haynes becomes the first black woman to publish an article in the *Journal of Negro History*, "Negroes in Domestic Service in the U.S." (Volume 8, October). Mary McLeod Bethune becomes the first black woman to deliver a major paper at an ASNLH annual meeting.

1924: The *Washington Tribune* publishes three articles on Woodson and the ASNLH.

1925: According to a *Washington Post* article from September 6, in Woodson's office-home, the ASNLH "presented an exhibition of 'engravings of the antique work of Benin, together with rare books and manuscripts.'" The *Washington Tribune* publishes four articles on Woodson and the ASNLH. Charles H. Wesley becomes the third African American to earn a PhD in history from Harvard. On March 23, Anna Julia Cooper becomes the first African American woman to earn a PhD in history (at Sorbonne in Paris).

1926: Inaugurates Negro History Week; receives the NAACP's Spingarn Medal; hires Zora Neale Hurston as a researcher. *Time* magazine has a column on Woodson under the heading "National Affairs." The Laura Spelman Rockefeller Fund renews and increases Woodson's grant. The Carnegie Corporation donates $10,000 to the New York Public Library for the buying of Schomburg's collection.

1927: Establishes the ASNLH's Extension Division, the Lecture Bureau and the Home Study Department.

1928: In February, receives a $16,000 grant from the Institute of Social and Religious Research and a $4,000 grant from the Social Science Research Council; travels to Cuba for research purposes. Lorenzo Johnston Greene works closely with Woodson as a researcher for the ASNLH and maintains a detailed diary of his experiences.

1929–33: Establishes the Woodson Collection at the Library of Congress.

1930: Helps found the Committee for Improving Industrial Conditions Among Negroes in the District of Columbia.

1931–36: Publishes more than one hundred articles/columns in the *New York Age*.

1932: Publishes about four articles/columns in the *Pittsburgh Courier*, one of which challenges sexual harassment within the black community; publishes first autobiographical sketch in the *New York Age*.

1932, 1933, 1935, 1937: Spends summers in Europe, vacationing and collecting documents pertaining to African history.

1932: Publishes approximately thirty-two articles/columns in the *Chicago Defender*.

1934: On November 30, creates a will and bequeaths the possession of the property of his office-home to the ASNLH upon his death. W. Sherman Savage receives a PhD in history from Ohio State University.

1935: Woodson initiates a $30,000 fundraising drive. Of the approximately two thousand history PhD degrees that have been awarded in the United States, only six went to African Americans. Lucy Harth Smith and Mary McLeod Bethune become the first black women elected to the ASNLH's executive council.

1936: Alrutheus A. Taylor and Rayford W. Logan receive PhD degrees in history from Harvard University.

1937: Woodson creates the *Negro History Bulletin* in October. James Hugo Johnston and Luther Porter Jackson receive PhD degrees in history from the University of Chicago.

1938–49: Woodson's debts surpassed his income.

1940: Eighteen African Americans have earned doctorates in history in the United States since 1895. Benjamin Quarles receives a PhD degree in history. Marion Thompson becomes the first African American woman to earn a PhD in history in the United States (at Columbia University).

1941: Woodson receives Doctor of Laws from West Virginia State College. John Hope Franklin receives a PhD in history from Harvard. Lulu M. Johnson, the second black woman to earn a PhD in history in the United States, receives her doctorate from Iowa State University.

1941–50: Woodson publishes approximately fifty-seven essays in the *Negro History Bulletin.*

1942: Lorenzo Johnston Greene receives a PhD in history from Columbia University.

1943: Susie Owen Lee receives a PhD in history from New York University.

1946: Elsie Lewis receives a PhD in history from the University of Chicago. Helen G. Edmonds receives a PhD in history from Ohio State University. Margaret Nelson Rowley receives a PhD in history from Columbia University.

1948: Woodson first introduces "Negro History Week Kits" at two dollars apiece.

1950: Woodson dies suddenly from a heart attack on April 3. Three other major figures in the black struggle for social justice and equality also die in 1950: Charles Drew, Charles Hamilton Houston and Luther Porter Jackson.

1951: In February, during Negro History Week, blacks in Chicago hold a formal Memorial Service for Woodson.

1958: Elected as "the third distinguished American" named to "The *Ebony* Hall of Fame" by readers.

1965: At the semicentennial celebration of the ASNLH at the fiftieth annual meeting in Atlanta from October 21–23, there is an hour-and-a-half-long opening session (the "Carter G. Woodson Memorial Session") in which Woodson is remembered by those who knew him well.

1971: The association no longer uses the Woodson Home as its headquarters. While in November it listed 1538 Ninth Street, Northwest, as its headquarters, by December it has changed its mailing address to 1407 Fourteenth Street, Northwest, Washington, D.C.

1972: The Association for the Study of Negro Life and History (ASNLH) changes its name to the Association for the Study of Afro-American Life and History (ASALH).

1974: On December 19, the Association for the Study of Afro-American Life and History renamed its new headquarters in honor of Carter G. Woodson.

1975: In December at the Third Liberty Baptist Church, about 150 yards away from Woodson's birthplace, the ASALH and the Amoco Foundation of Chicago place a bronze marker at the birthplace of Woodson.

1976: The former headquarters of the ASNLH at 1538 Ninth Street, Northwest, Washington, D.C., is designated a National Historic Landmark on May 11 (National Register #76002135). The ASALH creates Black History Month to replace Negro History Week.

1979: Woodson's home is listed in the District of Columbia's Inventory of Historic Sites on March 3.

1984: In commemoration of Woodson, the U.S. Postal Service issues a stamp of the ASNLH founder as a part of its Black Heritage Series.

1991: The Afro-American Institute for Historic Preservation and Community Development and the Institute for Urban Development Research at George Washington University produce the "Carter G. Woodson National Historic Site and Management Study."

1994: Mayor of West Virginia Robert Nelson erects a life-size statue of Woodson on Hal Greer Boulevard in Huntington, West Virginia.

1998: The Papers of Carter G. Woodson and the Association for the Study of Negro Life and History, 1915–1950, is processed and released as thirty-four microfilm reels. Emcee, soulful R&B singer and former member of the Fugees Lauryn Hill's debut and Grammy Award–winning album, *The Miseducation of Lauryn Hill*, is released, sampling from Woodson's classic *The Mis-Education of the Negro*.

1999: On November 2, Norton introduces the "Carter G. Woodson Home National Historic Site Study Act of 1999" in the House of Representatives.

2000: The value of Woodson's extensive collection of black history scholarship, documents and memorabilia is appraised at $600,000 to $1 million. On February 15, H.R. 3201 is approved and passed, 413–1, resulting in the "Carter G. Woodson Home National Historic Site Study Act of 2000." The Committee on Energy and National Resources authorizes the secretary of the interior "to prepare a resource study of the home of Dr. Carter G. Woodson to determine the suitability and feasibility of designating it as a unit of the National Park Service."

2001: The Carter G. Woodson Home is placed on the National Trust for Historic Preservation's list of "11 Most Endangered Places in the U.S."

2003: Based on Public Law 108-192, 117 Stat. 2873, signed on December 19, the National Park Service is authorized to acquire the Carter G. Woodson Home to establish a National Historic Site.

2004: Emory University acquires the Carter G. Woodson archives and places them within the university's Special Collections and Archives Division.

2005: On June 10, the National Park Service purchases the Woodson Home from ASALH for $465,000. The Woodson Home becomes the property of the NPS. Woodson's unpublished manuscript, "The Case of the Negro," is rediscovered by Daryl Scott (later republished as *Carter G. Woodson's Appeal* in 2008).

2009: John Hope Franklin, the last surviving professionally trained black historian who knew and worked with Woodson, dies on March 25 of congestive heart failure.

NOTES

PREFACE

1. Dean Gordon B. Hancock, "Between the Lines," *Los Angeles Sentinel,* March 13, 1947, 7.
2. Lorenzo Johnston Greene, "Dr. Carter G. Woodson: The Man as I Knew Him," typescript, n.d., Papers of Lorenzo Johnston Greene, container 92, folder 1, Manuscript Division, Library of Congress.
3. Charles H. Wesley, "Carter G. Woodson—As a Scholar," *Journal of Negro History* [hereafter *JNH*] 36 (January 1951): 12.

INTRODUCTION

4. Carter G. Woodson to Lorenzo Johnston Greene, 23 March 1945, Papers of Lorenzo Johnston Greene, container 74, folder 8, Manuscript Division, Library of Congress. Italics mine. Woodson used the phrase "willing to sacrifice" elsewhere.
5. Jacqueline Goggin, "Introduction," in Daniel Lewis, *A Guide to the Microfilm Edition of Papers of Carter G. Woodson and the Association for the Study of Negro Life and History, 1915–1950* (Bethesda, MD, 1999), xi.

According to Goggin, in the early 1920s, Woodson "purportedly" had a relationship with one of his secretaries, Alethe Smith.

6. Sister Anthony Scally, *Carter G. Woodson: A Bio-Bibliography* (Westport, CT: Greenwood Press, 1985), 12.
7. W. Montague Cobb, "Carter Godwin Woodson," *Negro History Bulletin* (hereafter cited as *NHB*) 36 (November 1963): 155.
8. Carter G. Woodson, "Carter Woodson Tells Reason Why He Never Married," *Pittsburgh Courier*, January 7, 1933, A2.
9. "Statement of Hon. Eleanor Holmes Norton, Delegate from the District of Columbia," *Hearing Before the Subcommittee on National Parks of the Committee on Energy and Natural Resources, United States Senate,* 108th Congress, 1st sess., S. 499, S. 546, S. 643, S. 677, S. 1060, H.R. 255, H.R. 1012, S. H.R. 1577, June 10, 2003 (Washington, D.C.: Government Printing Office, 2003), 5–6.
10. "Historical News," *JNH* 43 (January 1958): 82.
11. "Annual Report of the Director," *JNH* 26 (October 1941): 420.
12. "Negro History Week Literature Still Literature," *NHB* 3 (February 1940): 72.
13. "Negro History Week Celebrated February 10–17, 1946," *NHB* 9 (December 1945): 71.
14. "Annual Report," *JNH* 34 (October 1949): 384–85.
15. Greene, "Dr. Carter G. Woodson."

Chapter 1

16. *Chicago Defender*, "The Personal History of a Historian," March 6, 1937, 17.
17. Michael R. Winston, "Carter Godwin Woodson: Prophet of Black Tradition," *JNH* 60 (October 1975): 460.
18. *Norfolk Journal and Guide*, "The Poverty of the Depression Not Alarming—Woodson, Quoting Many," April 2, 1932, 7.
19. Greene, "Dr. Carter G. Woodson."
20. Woodson, "Carter Woodson Tells Reason Why He Never Married," A2.
21. *Norfolk Journal and Guide*, "Poverty of the Depression Not Alarming—Woodson, Quoting Many," 7.
22. Ibid., "Woodson and His Co-Workers Take the Vow of Poverty to Help Race," January 7, 1933.

23. Lorenzo Johnston Greene, "Dr. Woodson Prepares for Negro History Week, 1930," *NHB* 13 (May 1950): 195.

24. Langston Hughes, "When I Worked for Dr. Woodson," *NHB* 13 (May 1950): 188.

25. Greene, "Dr. Carter G. Woodson."

26. *Norfolk Journal and Guide*, "Carter G. Woodson Refutes Report About His Health," February 27, 1926, 1.

27. Scally, *Carter G. Woodson*, ix.

28. Greene, "Dr. Carter G. Woodson."

29. Carter G. Woodson, "And the Negro Loses His Soul," *Chicago Defender*, June 25, 1932, 14.

30. Scally, *Carter G. Woodson*, 4.

31. Woodson, "And the Negro Loses His Soul."

32. Carter G. Woodson, "Negroes Not United for Democracy," *NHB* 6 (May 1943): 170, 177; ibid., "In Spite of No Leaders the Negroes Hope for Democracy Lingers," 194, 213.

33. Ibid., "Negro Historians of Our Times," *NHB* 8 (April 1945): 155.

34. Ibid., "Early Education in West Virginia," *JNH* 7 (January 1922): 27.

35. Sister Anthony Scally, "The Philippines Challenge," *NHB* 44 (1981): 16–18.

36. Carter G. Woodson, "Carter G. Woodson in Fervid Plea for Nannie Burroughs," *Pittsburgh Courier*, May 14, 1932, A2.

37. Herbert Aptheker, ed., *Book Reviews by W.E.B. Du Bois* (New York: KTO Press, 1977), 67–68. Du Bois' review of *The Negro Church* was originally published in the *Freeman* on October 4, 1922, 92–93.

38. Greene, "Dr. Carter G. Woodson."

39. "The First Biennial Meeting of the Association for the Study of Negro Life and History at Washington," *JNH* 2 (October 1917): 445.

40. Carter G. Woodson, "Ten Years of Collecting and Publishing the Records of the Negro," *JNH* 10 (October 1925): 598.

41. Carter G. Woodson, "Association on Guard," *Norfolk Journal and Guide*, October 17, 1936, 8.

42. "$30,000 NEEDED," *JNH* 32 (January 1932): front matter.

43. "Notes," *JNH* 4 (April 1919): 237.

44. Ibid. (October 1919): 474; ibid., *JNH* 5 (January 1920): 135.

45. *New York Amsterdam News*, "Carter Woodson Refuses to Speak from the Same Platform as Pres. Durkee," November 18, 1925.

46. Patricia Romero, "Carter G. Woodson: A Biography" (PhD diss., Ohio State University, 1971), 129–130.

NOTES TO PAGES 52-61

47. Greene, "Dr. Carter G. Woodson."

48. L.D. Reddick, "As I Remember Woodson," *NHB* (November 1953): 36.

49. *Afro-American*, "Dr. Carter G. Woodson," November 8, 1930, 6.

50. Jacqueline Goggin, *Carter G. Woodson: A Life in Black History* (Baton Rouge: Louisiana State University Press, 1993), 174.

51. Carter G. Woodson, "Dr. Woodson Urges Voters in Next Election to Use Ballots Discriminately," *Atlanta Daily World*, September 16, 1932, 6.

52. Ibid., "Principle Is the Thing in Politics, Says Woodson," September 22, 1932, A2.

53. "Notes," *JNH* 9 (April 1924): 239.

54. Goggin, *Carter G. Woodson*, 94.

55. Darlene Clark Hine, *Hine Sight: Black Women and the Re-Construction of American History* (Brooklyn, NY, 1994), 221.

56. Goggin, *Carter G. Woodson*, 94.

57. "Annual Review," *JNH* 34 (October 1949): 383.

58. Cobb, "Carter Godwin Woodson," 155.

59. John Hope Franklin, "The Place of Carter G. Woodson in American Historiography," *NHB* 13 (May 1950): 175.

60. Albert N.D. Brooks, "Dr. Woodson the Inspiration," *NHB* 20 (December 1956): 66.

61. *Pittsburgh Courier (Washington Edition)*, "Noted Historian Gave Meaning to Past of Negroes," April 8, 1950.

62. *The Call*, "Death to Carter G. Woodson, Historian," April 14, 1950, 20.

63. Henry Arthur Callis, "Carter G. Woodson," *Washington Post*, April 8, 1950, 6.

64. Greene, "Dr. Carter G. Woodson."

65. "Proceedings of ASNLH Executive Council Meeting," April 8, 1950, Reel #3, Papers of Carter G. Woodson and the Association for the Study of Negro Life and History (Bethesda, MD, 1998).

66. Rayford W. Logan, "Report of the Director," *JNH* 35 (October 1950): 359.

67. Greene, "Dr. Carter G. Woodson."

68. *Chicago Defender*, "Set 1st History Meet Since Woodson's Death," September 30, 1950, 2.

69. Reddick, "As I Remember Woodson," 38.

NOTES TO PAGES 62–68

70. "Negro History Week Aftermath," *NHB* 10 (April 1947): 154, 165.

71. Eleanor Holmes Norton, "Foreword," in *The Black Washingtonians: The Anacostia Museum Illustrated Chronology*, edited by Smithsonian Anacostia Museum and Center for African American History and Culture (Hoboken, NJ, 2005), vii.

72. Kathryn S. Smith, "Remembering U Street," *Washington History* 9 (Fall/Winter 1997–98): 32.

73. Michael Andrew Fitzpatrick, "'A Great Migration for Business': Black Economic Development in Shaw," *Washington History* 2 (Fall/Winter 1990–91): 49.

74. Smith, "Remembering U Street," 31.

75. Michele F. Pacifico, "'Don't Buy Where You Can't Work': The New Negro Alliance of Washington," *Washington History* 6 (Spring/Summer 1994): 70.

76. For a sharp contrast to black life in the Shaw neighborhood, see William Henry Jones, *The Housing of Negroes in Washington, D.C.: A Study in Human Ecology* (Washington, D.C., 1929); James Borchert, *Alley Life in Washington: Family, Community, Religion, and Folklife in the City, 1850–1970* (Urbana, IL, 1982). According to Jones's findings, in 1925 there were 12,867 blacks in D.C.'s alleys and only 381 whites. The total black population in 1925 was 126,933, and the white population was 345,119.

77. Steven Mintz, "A Historical Ethnography of Black Washington, D.C.," *Records of the Columbia Historical Society* 52 (1989): 239.

78. Carter G. Woodson, "The 'Highly Educated' Quickly Graduated from the Methodist and Baptist Churches," *Afro-American* (Baltimore), March 28, 1931, 3.

79. *Pittsburgh Courier*, "Woodson Says 'Washington Has More Fool Negroes Than Any Other City,'" June 9, 1934, 5.

80. Fitzpatrick, "'Great Migration for Business,'" 50.

81. "The First Biennial Meeting of the Association for the Study of Negro Life and History at Washington," *JNH* 2 (October 1917): 442.

82. Marvin Caplan, "Eat Anywhere!: A Personal Recollection of the Thompson's Restaurant Case and the Desegregation of Washington's Eating Places," *Washington History* 1 (Spring 1989): 26.

83. Constance Green, *The Secret City: A History of Race Relations in the Nation's Capital* (Princeton, NJ, 1967), 201.

84. Goggin, *Carter G. Woodson*, 153.

85. *Washington Post*, "Negro Work Status in District Bared," March 26, 1932, 18.

86. Carter G. Woodson, "Accuses C.&O. of Humiliating Negro Patrons," *Norfolk Journal and Guide*, December 10, 1932, 2.

87. Greene, "Dr. Carter G. Woodson."

88. Carter G. Woodson, "Time and Foolhardiness Have Proved B.T. Washington's Joke a Prophecy—Woodson," *Norfolk Journal and Guide*, November 30, 1933, 7.

89. Carter G. Woodson, "Friday, 13th Unlucky to Carter Woodson, Who Is Held Up and Robbed," *Afro-American* (Baltimore), January 28, 1933, 7.

90. Ibid.

91. Cobb, "Carter Godwin Woodson," 153–55.

92. Residence of the Phyllis Wheatley Y.W.C.A., "The Death of the Founder," *NHB* 13 (May 1950): 176.

93. "Dr. Woodson to Be Buried Saturday," *Afro-American* (Washington), April 8, 1950.

94. Sister M. Anthony Scally, R.S.M., "Pioneer Black Historian," *Community* (Winter 1970): 12.

95. *Washington Post*, "1,000 Colored Children in Capitol Pilgrimage," February 11, 1932, 5.

96. "Negro History Week Assembly—A Suggestion for Middle Grades," *NHB* 5 (February 1942): 120.

97. "Negro History Week Aftermath," *NHB* 10 (April 1947): 154, 165.

98. "The Preparation of the Negro History Week Pamphlet for the Celebration, February 6–13," *NHB* 12 (January 1949): 88.

99. *Chicago Defender*, "Impressive Rites for Dr. Woodson," April 15, 1950, 4.

100. Carter G. Woodson, "Historian Claims He Was Misquoted," *Chicago Defender*, February 23, 1935, 5. For context, see *Afro-American* (Baltimore), "Scrap All Religion Woodson Tells 3,000 Detroiters," February 9, 1935, 10; *Chicago Defender*, "R.R. Wright, Sr. Answers Dr. Carter G. Woodson," March 9, 1935, 14.

101. "Negro History Week," *NHB* 9 (March 1946): 134–35; "Negro History Week Nation-Wide," *NHB* 12 (March 1949): 134.

102. Carter G. Woodson, "'Highly Educated' Quickly Graduated," *Afro-American* (Baltimore), March 28, 1931, 3. For a provocative discussion of Woodson's relationship with Burroughs, see Sharon Harley, "Nannie Helen Burroughs: 'The Black Goddess of Liberty,'" *JNH* 81 (Winter–Autumn 1996): 62–71.

103. "Negro History Week," *NHB* 8 (March 1945): 142.

104. Mabel Madden McCoy, review of *The Pastor's Voice* by Walter Henderson Brooks, *JNH* 31 (January 1946): 118.

105. "Negro History Week Aftermath," 165.

106. Jones, *Housing of Negroes in Washington, D.C.*, 94, 127.

107. "Notes," *JNH* 6 (July 1921): 380.

108. "Woodson and His Co-Workers," 9.

109. Carter G. Woodson, "Negro Writers Loafing," *Atlanta Daily World*, November 17, 1932, 6A.

110. Jacqueline Anne Goggin, "Carter G. Woodson and the Movement to Promote Black History" (PhD diss., University of Rochester, 1984), 286–87.

111. Katharine Capshaw Smith, *Children's Literature of the Harlem Renaissance* (Bloomington, IN, 2004), 164.

112. Rayford W. Logan, "Carter G. Woodson," *JNH* 35 (July 1950): 346.

113. Benjamin Quarles, "A Profile: The Associated Publishers," *NHB* 28 (January 1965): 81.

114. Greene, "Dr. Carter G. Woodson."

115. Jessie H. Roy, "Some Personal Recollections of Dr. Woodson," *NHB* 28 (Summer 1965): 186, 192.

116. Judith H. Robinson & Associates, Inc., "Developmental History," 33.

117. Goggin, "Carter G. Woodson and the Movement to Promote Black History," 280.

118. Ibid.

119. Hank Chase, "Carter G. Woodson's Home," *American Visions*, February 2000, http://findarticles.com/p/articles/mi_m1546/is_1_15/ai_59544562; Willie Leanna Miles, "Dr. Carter G. Woodson as I Recall Him, 1943–1950," *JNH* 76 (Winter–Autumn 1991): 96; Lorenzo J. Greene, *Working with Carter G. Woodson, the Father of Black History: A Diary, 1928–1930*, edited by Arvarh E. Strickland (Baton Rouge: Louisiana State University Press, 1989), 189; Greene, "Dr. Carter G. Woodson."

120. Woodson, "Time and Foolhardiness." Emphasis added.

121. Reddick, "As I Remember Woodson," 36.

122. Cobb, "Carter Godwin Woodson," 154–55.

123. Greene, "Dr. Carter G. Woodson."

124. Ibid., *Working with Carter G. Woodson*, 297.

125. Miles, "Dr. Carter G. Woodson as I Recall Him, 1943–1950," 92, 93, 95.

126. Judith H. Robinson & Associates, Inc., "Developmental History," 34.

127. "Current History," *NHB* 34 (March 1971): 59; "Contributions by ASNLH Clubs in Honor of Mother Gaston, Brooklyn, New York," ibid.; J. Rupert Picott, "Editorial Comment: Great and Good Tradition,"

NHB 36 (May 1973): 100; "Editorial Comment: America—The Third Century," *NHB* 39 (January 1976): 495.

128. Greene, "Dr. Carter G. Woodson."

129. Barry Mackintosh, *The Historic Sites Survey and National Historic Landmarks Programs: A History* (Washington, D.C., 1985).

130. "New Focus Projected for ASALH for 1980," *NHB* 42 (October–December 1979): 110.

131. J. Rupert Picott, "In This Bulletin," *NHB* 43 (April–June 1980): 27.

132. Judith H. Robinson & Associates, Inc., "Developmental History," 34.

133. For a discussion of Woodson's life in West Virginia and the Woodson statue there, see Ancella R. Bickley, "Carter G. Woodson: The West Virginia Connection," *Appalachian Heritage* 36 (Summer 2008): 59–69; Honorable Eleanor Holmes Norton, "Introduction of the Carter G. Woodson Home National Historic Site Study At of 1999," House of Representatives, November 2, 1999, http://bulk.resource.org/gpo.gov/record/1999/1999_E02249.pdf.

134. U.S. Congress, Senate, Committee on Energy and Natural Resources, *Carter G. Woodson Home National Historic Site Study Act of 2000*, 106th Congress, 2nd sess., Washington, D.C., June 27, 2000: 106–322.

135. Courtland Milloy, "Black History's Doorway Is in Need of Care," *Washington Post*, February 4, 2001, C01. Also see "Carter G. Woodson's Historic Home Is Now a Crackhouse," *Journal of Blacks in Higher Education* (Spring 2003): 60.

136. Executive Council, Association for the Study of African American Life and History, "Back Matter," *Journal of African American History* 88 (Summer 2003): 326.

137. "Carter G. Woodson Home National Historic Site," Committee on Energy and Natural Resources, Report, http://www.govnotes.com/Historic_Sites/_Carter_Woodson_Home_National_Historic.htm.

138. Ethan Gilsdorf, "Historic Highlights: Where Black History Began," *National Parks* 82 (Summer 2008): 58–59.

CHAPTER 3

139. Carter G. Woodson, "Negro History Week," *JNH* 11 (April 1926): 239.

140. Ibid., "The Celebration of Negro History Week, 1927," *JNH* 12 (April 1927): 105.

141. Ibid., "The Annual Report of the Director," (October 1927): 573.

142. Ibid., "Association on Guard," *Norfolk Journal and Guide*, October 17, 1936, 8.

143. "Negro History Week Aftermath," *NHB* 10 (April 1947): 153.

144. "Notes," *JNH* 4 (October 1919): 474.

145. Several historians seem to agree that the concept of Negro History Week originated in 1920. In that year, Woodson delivered a speech entitled "Democracy and the Man Far Down" to members of the Omega Psi Phi fraternity in Nashville, Tennessee. During the presentation, Woodson commented that these fraternity members needed to become more active in promoting the study of black life and history. The members of this Omega chapter responded by devoting one week out of every year to the study of black history. They called their celebration "Negro History and Literature Week." Their efforts continued until 1925. Woodson did not acknowledge the association's Negro History Week as an extension of the Omegas' efforts. For a discussion of the origins of Negro History Week, see Romero, "Carter G. Woodson: A Biography"; and Carter G. Woodson, "Negro History Week," *JNH* 11 (April 1926): 238–42.

146. Woodson, "Negro History Week," 238–41.

147. "Starting Right," *NHB* 1 (February 1938): 12; "Renew Your Subscription," *NHB* 9 (May 1946): 188.

148. "The Annual Report of the Director," *JNH* 11 (October 1926): 551.

149. Carter G. Woodson, "Start Now Negro History Year in Order to Have a Negro History Week," *NHB* 5 (October 1941): 24.

150. Woodson, "Negro History Week," 106–107.

151. L.D. Reddick, "Twenty-Five Negro History Weeks," *NHB* 13 (May 1950): 178–88; ibid., "Annual Report of the Director," *JNH* 18 (October 1933): 362.

152. Carter G. Woodson, *Home Study Department of the Extension Division of the ASNLH, Inc.: Bulletin of General Information* (Washington, D.C., no date).

153. Lillian M. Rhoades to Carter G. Woodson, November 14, 1940, Papers of Carter G. Woodson and the Association for the Study of Negro Life and History, Reel #1.

154. Carter G. Woodson, "Suggestion for Improving the Negro Church," *NHB* 3 (1939): 9.

155. Ibid., "The Negro Looks for Democracy," *NHB* 7 (December 1943): 72; ibid., "Why Negroes Fight in This War," (May 1944): 170.

156. John Hope Franklin, "Place of Carter G. Woodson in American Historiography," *NHB* 13 (May 1950): 176.

Chapter 4

157. Greene, *Working with Carter G. Woodson*, 198.

158. Miles, "Dr. Carter Godwin Woodson as I Recall Him," 95.

159. Greene, "Dr. Carter G. Woodson."

160. Ibid.

161. Wesley, "Carter G. Woodson—As Scholar," 12–24.

162. Reddick, "As I Remember Woodson," 36.

163. John Hope Franklin, "The New Negro History," *JNH* 43 (April 1957): 90–91, 93–94. The original article first appeared as "The New Negro History," *The Crisis* 64 (February 1957): 69–75.

164. Charles H. Wesley, "Our Fiftieth Year: Our Golden Anniversary, 1965," *NHB* 28 (May 1965): 173.

165. Roy, "Some Personal Recollection of Dr. Woodson," 186.

166. Lorenzo Johnston Greene, "Dr. Woodson Prepares for Negro History Week, 1930," *NHB* 28 (Summer 1965): 195.

167. Greene, "Dr. Carter G. Woodson."

168. Ibid.

169. Romero, "Carter G. Woodson," 95, 138, 185.

170. Rayford W. Logan, "Carter G. Woodson: Mirror and Molder of His Time, 1875–1950," *JNH* 58 (January 1973): 2.

171. Lorenzo Johnston Greene to Patricia Romero, April 25, 1984, Papers of Lorenzo Johnston Greene, container 27, folder 3; ibid., March 15, 1984, container 70, folder 8.

172. Marion J. Pryde, "My Personal and Family Reminiscences of Dr. Carter Godwin Woodson," *JNH* 76 (Winter-Autumn 1991): 101–05.

Epilogue

173. For a discussion of personality traits that I have cited from here, see "Definition of Personality Traits," http://www.yourdictionary.com/library/reference/define-personality-traits.html.

174. After Woodson died in 1950, L.D. Reddick referred to Woodson as the "Father of Negro History" in the essay "Twenty-Five Negro History Weeks," 178. During the 1950s and 1960s, Woodson was routinely called the "Father of Negro History." By the Black Power era, Woodson was referred to as the "Father of Black History." Now,

Woodson is universally called the "Father of Black History." The first references to Woodson as the "father of Negro history" were in the 1940s. See, for example, Mavis Mixon, "The Development of the Study of Negro History in Chicago," *Chicago Defender*, February 7, 1942, 15; a letter from Chicagoan Madeline R. Morgan in "Negro History Week," *NHB* (March 1945): 142.

175. Albert N.D. Brooks, "Carter Godwin Woodson School," *NHB* 16 (June 1953): 215–16.

176. "Carter G. Woodson Fund Report: Columbian Education Association Gives Help," *NHB* 15 (February 1952): 93, 103.

177. "The Carter G. Woodson History Club," *NHB* 12 (June 1949): 201, 215.

178. See *Washington Post*, "Negro History Week to Begin Tomorrow," February 7, 1926, R10; "Woodson Addresses Armstrong Students," October 9, 1927, R10; "Negro Chance Seen By Tuskegee Head," October 31, 1929, 10.

179. See, for instance, *Washington Post*, "Students Honor Carter Woodson," February 16, 1946, 5.

180. "Negro History Week," *NHB* 9 (March 1946): 134–36.

181. Ibid., 8 (March 1945): 142.

182. "The Fifteenth Celebration of Negro History Week," *NHB* 3 (March 1940): 88.

183. "Timely Suggestions for Negro History Week," *NHB* 1 (February 1938): 11.

184. "Negro History Week in Pictures," *NHB* 11 (January 1948): 85.

185. Carter G. Woodson, *The Mis-Education of the Negro* (Washington, D.C., 1933), 44, 131.

186. "Timely Suggestions for Negro History Week," 11.

SELECTED BIBLIOGRAPHY

The following brief list of secondary sources dealing with Woodson is by no means comprehensive. For further information regarding Woodson, as well as the issues explored in the chapters of this book, the sources referenced in the text as well as in the notes should be consulted. The sources listed below represent an abbreviated collection of insightful works pertaining to Woodson.

Burkett, Randall K., Pellom McDaniels III and Tiffany Gleason. *The Mind of Carter G Woodson as Reflected in the Books He Owned, Read, and Published: A Catalog of the Library of Carter G. Woodson and the Association for the Study of African American Life and History*. Atlanta, GA: Emory University, 2006.

Cobb, W. Montague. "Carter Godwin Woodson." *Negro History Bulletin* 36 (November 1973): 151–55.

Dagbovie, Pero Gaglo. *The Early Black History Movement, Carter G. Woodson, and Lorenzo Johnston Greene*. Urbana: University of Illinois Press, 2007.

Donaldson, Bobby J. "'Circles of Learning': Exploring the Library of Carter G. Woodson." *Journal of African American History* 93 (Winter 2008): 80–87.

Fenderson, Johnathon. "Evolving Conceptions of Pan-African Scholarship: W.E.B. Du Bois, Carter G. Woodson & the Encyclopedia Africana, 1909–1963." *Journal of African American History* 95 (Winter 2010): 71–91.

Franklin, John Hope. "The Place of Carter G. Woodson in American Historiography." *Negro History Bulletin* 13 (May 1950): 174–76.

Goggin, Jacqueline. *Carter G. Woodson: A Life in Black History*. Baton Rouge: Louisiana State University Press, 1993.

Greene, Lorenzo J. *Selling Black History for Carter G. Woodson: A Diary, 1930–1933*. Edited by Arvarh E. Strickland. Columbia: University of Missouri Press, 1996.

———. *Working with Carter G. Woodson, the Father of Black History: A Diary, 1928–1930*. Edited by Arvarh E. Strickland. Baton Rouge: Louisiana State University Press, 1989.

Hine, Darlene Clark. "Carter G. Woodson: White Philanthropy and Negro Historiography." *History Teacher* 19 (May 1986): 405–25.

Judith H. Robinson & Associates, Inc. "Developmental History." In *Carter G. Woodson Home: Historic Structure Report, Contract No. C3000600016/NPS PMIS Reference No. 125623*. Prepared by Beyer Blinder Belle, Architects & Planners, LLP, January 15, 2008, 10–63.

King, LaGarrett J., Ryan M. Crowley and Anthony L. Brown. "The Forgotten Legacy of Carter G. Woodson: Contributions to Multicultural Social Studies and African American History." *Social Studies* 101 (2010): 211–15.

Logan, Rayford W. "Carter G. Woodson: Mirror and Molder of His Times, 1875–1950." *Journal of Negro History* 58 (1973): 1–17.

Martin, Tony. "Carter G. Woodson and Marcus Garvey." *Negro History Bulletin* 40 (November–December 1977): 774–77.

Meier, August, and Elliott Rudwick. *Black History and the Historical Profession, 1915–1980*. Urbana: University of Illinois Press, 1986.

———. "J. Franklin Jameson, Carter G. Woodson, and the Foundations of Black Historiography." *American Historical Review* 89 (October 1984): 1005–15.

Miller, Kelly. *An Estimate of Carter G. Woodson and His Work in Connection with the Association for the Study of Negro Life and History, Inc.* Washington, D.C.: ASNLH, 1926.

Reddick, L.D. "Carter G. Woodson (1875–1950): An Appreciation." *Phylon* 11 (1950): 177–79.

Romero, Patricia. "Carter G. Woodson: A Biography." PhD diss., Ohio State University, 1971.

Scally, M.A. *Walking Proud: The Story of Dr. Carter G. Woodson*. Washington, D.C.: Associated Publishers, 1983.

Scally, Sister Anthony. *Carter G. Woodson: A Bio-Bibliography*. Westport, CT: Greenwood Press, 1985.

Scruggs, Ottey M. "Carter G. Woodson, the Negro History Movement, and Africa." *Pan African Journal* 7 (Spring 1974): 39–50.

Wesley, Charles H. "Carter G. Woodson—As a Scholar." *Journal of Negro History* 36 (1951): 12–24.

INDEX

ABOUT THE AUTHOR

Pero Gaglo Dagbovie is a professor in the Department of History at Michigan State University in East Lansing, Michigan. His books include *Black History: "Old School" Black Historians and the Hip Hop Generation* (Bedford Publishers, Inc., 2006), *The Early Black History Movement, Carter G. Woodson, and Lorenzo Johnston Greene* (University of Illinois Press, 2007), *African American History Reconsidered* (University of Illinois Press, 2010) and *What Is African American History?* (Polity Press, 2015). As the principal investigator for the Carter G. Woodson Home, NHS, he completed

the historic resource study entitled *"Willing to Sacrifice": Carter G. Woodson, the Father of Black History, and the Carter G. Woodson Home, NHS* (Washington, DC: National Park Service, U.S. Department of Interior, National Capital Region, 2010). He is a lifetime member of the Association for the Study of African American Life and History.

CPSIA information can be obtained
at www.ICGtesting.com
Printed in the USA
LVOW04*0741070318

568944LV00010B/51/P